# TALES OF OF MICHIGAN

*Constance M. Jerlecki*

## INLAND
## EXPRESSIONS

*Clinton Township, Michigan*

Published by Inland Expressions

Inland Expressions
42211 Garfield Rd. #297
Clinton Township, MI. 48038

www.inlandexpressions.com

First Edition 2012

ISBN-13  978-1-939150-00-4

Printed in the United States of America.

Design by Inland Expressions

# Table of Contents

# Preface

During the initial stages of developing this book, a decision was made to incorporate a broad range of stories from across the state rather than concentrating on any single aspect of Michigan's history or geographical region. Therefore, each chapter included in this book focuses on one particular subject matter, with an emphasis, in most cases, placed upon relating lesser known events and individuals that are components of Michigan's historical heritage.

Bordered by four of the five Great Lakes, it is fitting that Michigan gets its name from the word *Michigama*, which in the Algonquin language means great or large lake. Understandably, Michigan has a rich maritime heritage, and thus it should come as no surprise that many of the stories incorporated into this volume have nautical components or themes.

The inspiration for one of the chapters included in this publication came about during the summer of 2007, when the author visited a small cemetery in St. Clair County. It was on this day that the discovery of an interesting inscription on one of the crumbling tombstones located in that cemetery later led to the conducting of the first research for this book.

The history of Michigan is a wide and diverse subject, and no work on the subject can ignore the contribution that industry has made in the economic evolution of the state. To this end, it was decided to relate the tale of how Detroit, widely regarded today as the "Automotive Capital of the World," was once home to a thriving stove industry. Michigan is a state of contrasts, and to illustrate this, it was felt appropriate to include a chapter devoted to a general history of Isle Royale, perhaps one of the most protected wilderness areas of the state.

While the fifteen stories included in this book can only be expected to scratch the surface of Michigan's rich and varied past, it is hoped that the reader gains some additional insight into the story of the "Great Lakes State" through the reading this book.

Constance M. Jerlecki
September 2012

# Chapter One
## Protecting a Vital Chokepoint

During the Second World War, the industrial might of the United States became focused upon the production of war materials. This was especially true for the domestic steel industry that, after enduring the lean years of the Great Depression, responded vigorously to the increasing demands brought about by the war. To manufacture their products, the steel mills required large amounts of iron ore, coal, and limestone, all of which were capable of being efficiently transported on the Great Lakes.

There is, however, one major obstacle in shipping iron ore from ports on Lake Superior to destinations on the lower lakes. This was the fact that water level of Lake Superior is 21 feet higher than that of Lake Huron, to which it connects via the St. Marys River. Such a difference in height created a series of rapids in the St. Marys River between Sault Ste. Marie, Michigan, and a city on the Canadian side of the river that shares an identical name. These rapids prevented the direct shipment of cargoes from Lake Superior and led to a practice of unloading cargoes at Sault Ste. Marie above the rapids that would then be transported across land and reloaded into vessels below the rapids at the Lake Huron level. This inefficient practice remained in common use until the opening of the State Locks on June 18, 1855. On that date, the steamer *Illinois*, commanded by Captain Jack Wilson, became the first ship to use the new canal when it passed upbound into Lake Superior.[1]

The first shipment of iron ore through the locks at Sault Ste. Marie occurred on August 17, 1855, when the brig *Columbia* transited the canal with 132 tons of ore consigned to the Cleveland Iron Mining Co., which had been loaded at Marquette.[2] Following this pioneering shipment, the transportation of ore through the locks at Sault Ste. Marie grew at an almost unbelievable rate as the mining and shipping industries struggled to meet the demands of the hungry blast furnaces of a growing nation. By 1900, the transportation of iron ore on the Great Lakes had grown to 18,570,315 gross tons, a respectable figure considering that winter limited the shipping season on the lakes to only eight months in length.

Originally controlled by the State of Michigan, the Federal Government assumed the responsibility for the St. Marys Falls Ship Canal on June 6, 1881. Following this, all ships transiting the locks were permitted to do so without being charged tolls, a practice that continues to this day. Steadily increasing ship

A photograph of the original State Locks, which opened in 1855. (US Army Corps of Engineers)

With the Weitzel Lock on the left, and the original Poe Lock to the right, improvements made to the locks at Sault Ste. Marie during the late nineteenth century are readily apparent in this view. (Michigan Technological University Archives and Copper Country Historical Collections)

traffic through the canal led to the construction of a larger lock that opened on September 4, 1881. Originally known simply as the "New Lock," this lock was named the Weitzel Lock in 1896 to honor US Army General Godfrey Weitzel. In that same year, a third lock, the original Poe Lock, also opened to traffic. Built on the site of the original State Locks, this lock measured 800 feet long and 100 feet wide.

During 1895, the Canadian Government opened its own lock across the river from the Soo Locks at Sault Ste. Marie, Ontario. One of the reasons behind the construction of this lock resulted from an incident that occurred in May 1879 when a Canadian vessel, the *Chicora*, loaded with troops and military supplies bound to quell the Riel Rebellion in Manitoba was refused passage through the US Government controlled locks. A further

3

A photograph showing vessels along the lower approach wall, awaiting their turn to enter the Soo Locks in order to be raised to the Lake Superior level, ca. 1890s. (Bayliss Public Library)

reason was a threat by the United States during the 1880s to levy tolls against ships passing through the Soo Locks bound for ports in Canada. This was in retaliation for tolls being charged by the Canadian Government for vessels transiting the Welland Canal, which connects Lakes Erie and Ontario.[3]

Two further locks entered service during the early part of the twentieth century. These were the Davis and Sabin Locks, which entered operation on October 21, 1914 and September 18, 1919 respectively. Each of these locks measured 1,350 feet in length and 80 feet in width. As the largest ships on the Great Lakes at that time measured no more than 625 feet in length, it was possible to lock through at least two vessels simultaneously.

By the beginning of World War I in 1914, the iron ore trade on the Great Lakes had reached 32,021,897 gross tons, which had nearly doubled by the end of that conflict in 1918 to 61,156,732 gross tons.[4] As can be expected, the onset of the Great Depression in 1929 had an adverse impact on the shipment of raw materials on the inland seas. The worse year, in terms of iron ore carriage, during this timeframe was 1932, which saw

A company of troops assembles for inspection at Fort Brady, ca. 1908. (Library of Congress)

only 3,567,985 tons of that commodity being transported on the lakes during that shipping season.

By the late 1930s, however, cargoes became more plentiful as the economic situation improved. On September 1, 1939, German forces invaded Poland, thus heralding the beginning of the Second World War. While the United States was officially neutral during the early stages of this conflict, the strategic importance of the Soo Locks required defensive measures to be taken in order to protect them. Up to this time, visitors had been given relatively unfettered access to the four locks. This quickly changed following the onset of war as within one week of Hitler's invasion of Poland, the area surrounding the Soo Locks was closed to the public and armed troops began patrolling the area.[5]

As Sault Ste. Marie relied heavily upon tourism, the closure of the Soo Locks to visitors greatly alarmed many business owners and local officials. During the spring of 1940, Michigan Senator

The railroad bascule bridge crossing the St. Marys Falls Ship Canal is shown in the closed position. On October 7, 1941, a partial collapse of this bridge caused a steam locomotive to plunge into the canal, killing two. (Library of Congress)

Prentiss M. Brown and Representative Fred Bradley pressured the military to lift its ban on the locks.[6] Although the military rescinded its restrictions in June of that year, it later reversed this decision in August with the area around the locks being sealed off once again in early September, following the end of the tourist season.

The military had a long history in the area, with the first Fort Brady being established at Sault Ste. Marie in 1822 to deter British incursions from Canada. While the Army later abandoned this outpost, it was reformed in 1866 to provide protection for the St. Marys Falls Ship Canal. Located just downstream from the locks, this location was abandoned in 1893 with a new Fort Brady being reestablished at a spot approximately one mile southwest of the Soo Locks.

The vulnerability and importance of the Soo Locks became apparent on October 7, 1941 when a steam locomotive, and its tender, fell into the north canal when a leaf on the bascule bridge crossing just upstream from the locks collapsed. This accident immediately halted all ship traffic through the Davis and Sabin Locks. At the time, these two locks were the busiest of the four locks at Sault Ste. Marie as they both allowed ships drawing up to 20 feet in draft to pass. Of the two locks not effected by the accident, the Poe Lock was only able to handle ships drawing up to 16 ½ feet, while the Weitzel was obsolete, having not been used regularly since the end of World War I.

As can be expected, there was some initial concern that the bridge may have been sabotaged. This was quickly ruled out, however, as inspectors found no evidence that the accident had resulted from an intentional act. When the bridge collapsed, four persons on the train were thrown into the canal. Of these, the engineer, Hazel Willis of Gladstone and the conductor, David Monroe of Sault Ste. Marie were both drowned. Two other crewmembers, Carl Zelmer and Francis Peller were rescued from the water by soldiers from nearby Fort Brady.[7]

With the shipping canal blocked, a large number of freighters were affected, with several tying up to await the reopening of the locks. As the cargoes being transported through the Soo Locks were so vital to the nation's industrial sector, the news of the bridge accident made the front page of numerous newspapers across the nation. Compounded by the accident was the lateness of the shipping season that normally ended by mid-December with the onset of wintry conditions on the lakes. This meant that if the canal remained closed for a prolonged period, shipping fleets operating on the Great Lakes would be hard pressed to make up any losses in cargoes not moved while their ships were idled.

Realizing the importance of the Soo Locks, wrecking crews and army engineers immediately went to work clearing the canal of wreckage. Engaged in this task was the largest salvage tug on the Great Lakes, the *Favorite*. Within two days of the accident, the *Favorite* had been able to move the 120 ton locomotive and its tender to the side of the canal where it was lifted out of the water and placed on a scow. With the canal cleared, ship traffic was able to resume with more than 100 freighters waiting to transit the locks.[8]

Two months to the day following the train accident, Japanese naval forces attacked the US Navy's Pacific Fleet at Pearl Harbor, Hawaii, thus plunging the United States into the Second World War. This event placed an increased emphasis upon the security of the Soo Locks as reported in the December 8, 1941 edition of Marshall, Michigan's *The Evening Chronicle*:

> At Fort Brady, in the Upper Peninsula, commanding officer Lieut. Col. M. L. Soderholm tightened the guard over the important Soo Locks and instructed machine gunners at its locks and gates to remain on the alert constantly.

Four days following the Pearl Harbor Attack, Germany and Italy announced their declaration of war against the United States. While sabotage by enemy agents had been a concern since the fall of 1939, the fact that the United States and Germany were now at war presented the possibility of a direct attack against the Soo Locks by Axis military forces. It was surmised that Germany could mount such an attack by using one of three options.

The first two options would have included attacks mounted by long-range Luftwaffe attack aircraft using bombs or torpedoes. In order to permit the bombers to reach Sault Ste. Marie they could have been deployed in one of two ways. The first was to transport the aircraft broken down in surface ships or submarines that would sail into Hudson Bay. After being reassembled, the German aircraft would have had no difficulty in reaching the Soo Locks just 600 miles to the south. Another

Three barrage balloons are shown being deployed by the US Marine Corps at Parris Island, South Carolina in early 1942. Designed to frustrate enemy air attacks, balloons such as these were stationed around the Soo Locks during the Second World War. (Library of Congress)

scenario envisioned the possibility of launching the bomber aircraft from Nazi bases in occupied Norway. Flying the Great Circle route, Sault Ste. Marie was well within the range of such aircraft on one-way missions.

The third option for a Nazi attack on Sault Ste. Marie would have involved the insertion of paratroops in areas outside of the city. These forces would have then attacked the locks, possibly causing heavy damages by using demolition charges. This plan had a serious drawback, however, as the invading forces would have most likely been killed or taken prisoner despite whether or not their attack was successful. This would have produced a somewhat suicidal nature to such a plan. In an assessment done during the war, engineers estimated that it could take up to four months to get one lock operational following a successful enemy attack. Furthermore, it was estimated that it could take up to a year to bring all three locks back into service in the event that all had been damaged in an attack.[9]

While Germany possessed the material resources to conduct a direct aerial assault against the Soo Locks, the effectiveness of such an operation would have been questionable at best. Early concerns over the security of the locks, however, brought about the deployment of some 7,300 troops into the Sault Ste. Marie area by the end of 1942. This represented a sizable number for a city that the 1940 Census records as having a population of 15,847 residents.

Among the defensive measures taken to safeguard the infrastructure of the St. Marys Falls Ship Canal was the installation of anti-torpedo nets to protect the gates of the locks, and the deployment of a number of barrage balloons to hamper

On July 11, 1943, the steamer *Carl D. Bradley* makes the first commercial transit through the MacArthur Lock. (Author's Collection)

any attack by low-flying aircraft. Additionally, 60-inch diameter searchlights were installed in strategic locations around the locks, while a large number of civilian volunteers received training to act as aircraft spotters. To provide the capability to produce smokescreens for the vital installation, two companies of chemical warfare troops were also deployed to the area.[10]

Responding to the increased demands in tonnage passing through the Soo Locks, the US Congress authorized the construction of a new lock on March 7, 1942. This lock was to be built on the site of the defunct Weitzel Lock, with construction beginning in May of 1942.[11] With a length of 800 feet, the new lock was significantly shorter than the Davis and Sabin Locks both of which measured 1,350 feet long. Although shorter, the new lock retained the same width of 80 feet and was capable of handling deeper laden vessels. Through an act of Congress, the new lock was named to honor General Douglas MacArthur, thus deviating from the previous tradition of naming locks after officers belonging to the US Army Corps of Engineers. On July 11, 1943, just a little more than a year after the beginning of construction, the MacArthur Lock opened with the United States Steel's Bradley Transportation Division's steamer *Carl D. Bradley* making the first commercial passage.[12] When completed, the cost of the lock's construction amounted to $14 million, an expenditure nearly twice the original $8 million estimate.

As the shock of Pearl Harbor quieted, and the chances of a Nazi attack on the locks became more remote, the military began reducing the size of its garrison at Sault Ste. Marie. On May 25, 1943, the War Department cut the number of troops stationed in the area to just 2,000 personnel.[13] By early 1944, both the US and Canada had abandoned all of their aircraft warning stations. During the same timeframe, the US Army reduced its garrison at Fort Brady to a single battalion of military police, the same level as it had held prior to the United States entering the war.

Further personnel reductions during 1944 resulted in just a single company of troops stationed at Sault Ste. Marie by the end of the year.

The Second World War ended on August 15, 1945 with Japan's unconditional surrender. Following this, the military drawdown at the Soo Locks continued with the closure of Fort Brady in October of that year. This occurred despite the efforts of Michigan Governor Harry Kelly, and a delegation of officials from Sault Ste. Marie, whom petitioned the War Department in an effort to halt the closure of the fort.[14] In 1946, the Michigan College of Mining and Technology (later Lake Superior State University) converted the site of former Fort Brady into a college campus.

Although the Army left the area following the end of World War II, just five years later the protection of the Soo Locks once again became a national security priority with the beginning of the Korean War. Once again, an armed conflict placed enormous demands upon the Great Lakes shipping fleet in transporting

A historical marker erected upon the grounds of old Fort Brady at Sault Ste. Marie, just east of the Soo Locks. (Author's Photo)

raw materials through the Soo Locks for domestic steel production. In response, the US Army returned to Sault Ste. Marie in July 1950 and established Camp Lucas using buildings that were formerly the hospital at Fort Brady as its headquarters.

To deter an aerial attack against the Soo Locks infrastructure, the US Army's 8th Anti-Aircraft Battalion erected gun emplacements around the locks.[15] Additionally, the passage of tour boats through the Soo Locks, a popular tourist attraction back then as it is today, was prohibited. However, such vessels were able to continue operating by utilizing the Canadian Lock.

In 1952, the US Air Force reactivated Kinross Air Force Base just outside of Sault Ste. Marie. Established in 1943, this airfield was located some twenty miles south of Sault Ste. Mare in Kinross Township. In April 1953, the 438th Fighter Interceptor

A current view of the locks at Sault Ste. Marie, Michigan. This installation represents one of the most critical pieces of infrastructure for shipping on the Great Lakes. (US Army Corps of Engineers)

Squadron was activated at Kinross AFB. This squadron was initially equipped with F-94 Starfire jet interceptors, which were replaced during the summer of 1954 by F-89 Scorpion interceptors. In September 1959, Kinross AFB was renamed to Kincheloe Air Force Base in honor of Captain Iven Carl Kincheloe, Jr., a Michigan native killed in a crash of an F-104 Starfighter the previous year.

During 1960, the US Army deactivated Camp Lucas as it reduced its presence at Sault Ste. Marie. Meanwhile, the USAF continued its operations at Kincheloe AFB with the introduction of BOMARC anti-aircraft missile batteries and the 438th Fighter Interception Squadron's transition to operating long-range F-106 Delta Dart interceptors. Beginning in 1961, a number of B-52 Stratofortress bombers and KC-135 Stratotankers belonging to the Strategic Air Command were also based at Kincheloe following improvements being made to the airfield's runways.

In August 1968, the 438th Fighter Interceptor Squadron transferred from Kincheloe AFB to Griffiss AFB, New York. The departure of the fighter squadron, left the 449th Bombardment Wing as Kincheloe's host unit. The Air Force had originally planned to deactivate Kincheloe in 1971, however, political pressure kept the airbase open until it was finally shut down on September 30, 1977. Kincheloe survives today as the Chippewa County International Airport.

In 1968, a new lock capable of handling ships up to 1,000 feet in length and 105 feet in width was completed at Sault Ste. Marie. Built upon the site of the original Poe Lock that had entered service in 1896, the new lock would share the same name. This second Poe Lock allowed for the construction of significantly larger ships, which would transform US flagged shipping operations on the Great Lakes during the 1970s.

Following the terrorist attacks of September 11, 2001, the security of Soo Locks, and its infrastructure, was once again tightened in an attempt to prevent any terrorist acts. Despite a general downsizing in the industrial capability of the United States over the past thirty years, the Soo Locks continues to be an integral component of the Great Lakes and St. Lawrence Seaway systems. For example, during 2010 nearly 42 million tons of ore and just over 19 million tons of coal were shipped from ports on Lake Superior.[16] With the vast majority of these shipments consigned to destinations beyond the largest of the Great Lakes, the Soo Locks continues to fulfill the same vital function that led to the construction of the first locks at Sault Ste. Marie more than 150 years ago.

# Chapter Two
## The Midland Salt & Lumber Plant Explosion - 1892

Centrally located in Michigan's Lower Peninsula, Midland County was home to a thriving logging industry during the late 1800s. With an abundance of timber and several natural waterways, the region bordering the shores of Saginaw Bay was ideally suited for logging. While much of the lumber produced by this region was consumed in the building of the large cities bordering the Great Lakes such as Buffalo, Chicago, Cleveland, Detroit, and Milwaukee it was also shipped to the East Coast as forests in that part of the country were becoming depleted.

With plentiful game, fish, wild rice, and berries, the area that was to become Midland County had long been home to groups of Chippewa Indians. This same region was also abundant in beaver, the pelts of which were a valuable commodity until the mid-1800s. The pursuit of these pelts brought the first white settlers into Midland County during 1831. Shortly thereafter, a trading post was established by the American Fur Company at the junction of the Tittabawassee and Chippewa Rivers. It would be at this location that the founders of Midland would locate their village.

By 1850, the community of Midland had grown to 65 persons. That same year saw the formation of Midland County, although no elections for county officials would take place until 1855. The population of the county would grow in proportion to the expansion of the lumber industry, which reached its peak in 1880. During this time, it is said that there were lumber camps located nearly every four miles upon the county's waterways. This appears to be an accurate assessment as the 1878 Annual

Report of the Tittabawassee Boom Company identifies some 1,100 individual marks (each log was marked by the company that had harvested it) for logging companies operating in the Saginaw Valley. The rivers provided lumberjacks with a simple, and efficient, method for transporting their logs to the lumber mills for processing. Many such mills were located in nearby Bay City and Saginaw. Benefiting from an easy access to Saginaw Bay, and therefore all navigable points on the Great Lakes, these cities became two of the busiest ports on the lakes during this timeframe.

Besides lumber, Midland County sits atop a significant brine deposit. The harvesting of salt from brine has been widespread throughout Michigan since its earliest days. For example, between 1860 and 1868 some 3,282,681 barrels of salt was produced in the state. By 1890, the manufacture of salt on an

The logging industry played a key role in the growth of Michigan during the late 1800s and early 1900s. Here a stack of logs is awaiting transport to the lumber mill, ca. 1880-1899. (Library of Congress)

annual basis in Michigan had grown to 3,838,637 barrels.[1] The presence of plentiful chemical brines in the county led to the founding of the Dow Chemical Company at Midland in 1897.

With its brine deposits and burgeoning logging industry, Midland County attracted large numbers of workers, and their families, to settle in the area. By 1874, the Flint and Pere Marquette Railroad had laid the first railway line in the village of Midland. Responding to its growth, the city of Midland was incorporated in 1887. A few years later, during the waning days of the timber boom in this part of the state, the peaceful surroundings of this growing community was shattered by an accident at one of its lumber mills.

On the afternoon of May 12, 1892, workers had just returned to their duties at the Midland Salt and Lumber plant when the facility's four boilers suddenly exploded. The explosion killed four workers and seriously injured eleven more, and resulted in the complete destruction of the mill and salt block (a salt factory that uses an evaporation process).

Killed in the explosion were John Allen, A. L. Malcom, Richard Stears, and Eugene Van Valkenberg. The blast was powerful enough that Allen and Van Valkenberg were both thrown some 100 feet through the air from where the boilers once stood, their bodies terribly mutilated.[2] As can be expected, the boilers themselves were blown to bits.

The boiler explosion occurred at 1:35 in the afternoon, just after workers at the plant had returned from their lunch break. As the mill employed 75 workers at the time of the accident, it was fortunate that a majority of those present were able to escape without injury. Below is an excerpt from a news story printed in the *Logansport Daily Reporter* on May 13, 1892:

### Without Warning

The survivors have little to tell, as the explosion came without warning. They simply remember a terrible shock and the feeling as though falling a great distance. Then came a moment's silence, broken by screams, groans and curses, as the wounded and pinioned men began to feel their hurts and realize their positions.

Immediately following the accident, newspapers began reporting that the owners of the Midland Salt & Lumber plant had come under fire by claims that they had known the boilers operated at the plant were defective. Regardless of the legitimacy of such accusations, the plant was completely wrecked by the explosion. At the time of the incident, the mill and salt block were valued at $50,000.[3]

Boiler explosions were a somewhat common occurrence during this era. Operating with extreme pressures, such installations can be extremely dangerous and unforgiving as the smallest mistake or mechanical defect will often lead to disastrous consequences. In fact, just a little less than two months earlier, on March 21, 1892, a similar boiler explosion ripped through a lumber mill in East Jordan, near Charlevoix. Although this accident did not completely destroy the mill as had occurred in the Midland blast, it left at least six workers dead and many others seriously injured.[4]

# Chapter Three
## Train Collision at Battle Creek - 1893

Named for a skirmish that took place between government land surveyors and a pair of Potawatomi Indians in 1825, the city of Battle Creek is located in southwestern Michigan 110 miles west of Detroit. The first permanent settlers arrived in the area during 1831 and within ten years, the village, originally known as Milton, had become a trading center for area farmers. In 1859, the growing city, and one-day cereal capital of the world, changed its name to Battle Creek. It would be in this city during 1893 that one of the worst train wrecks in Michigan history would occur.

The first train to arrive at Battle Creek chugged its way into the city during December of 1845. Arriving one week later than originally planned, the wood burning steam locomotive was greeted only by a small crowd of onlookers. Despite its less than auspicious arrival, the train quickly became the focus of much attention as it performed its duties on the newly laid tracks.[1]

When first proposed, the rail line through Battle Creek had met heavy opposition from local farmers concerned that their oxen could not get out of the way of a steam locomotive traveling at 12 miles per hour. This dispute was quickly settled, however, when surveyors working out the route of the rail line threatened to run it through Battle Creek's rival in commerce, the village of Verona, instead.[2]

The arrival of the railroads allowed the farmers and industries located in the Battle Creek area to find new markets for their products. This increase in commerce helped to fuel the growth of the city, which by the later years of the nineteenth century had a population in excess of 22,000 inhabitants.

At 8:15 in the evening of Thursday October 19, 1893, a Raymond and Whitcomb special excursion train departed the Sixtieth Street Station at Chicago bound for the East Coast.[3] Operated by the Chicago & Grand Trunk Railway, and known as the No. 6, this train consisted of a locomotive and eight coaches. Having spent time in Chicago attending the World's Fair, the passengers aboard this train were on their return journey to New York and Boston.

As the No. 6 continued its way eastbound, it neared the city of Battle Creek, where it was scheduled to make a stop. Arriving there around 3:35 on the morning of October 20, 1893, the train's conductor, Bertram Scott, received two copies of a dispatch from the night operator ordering the No. 6 to proceed to the double tracks east of Main Street, a distance of about half a mile. Here the No. 6 was to await the passage of a westbound train, the Pacific Express No. 9, before continuing onwards.

After receiving these orders, the engineer of the Raymond and Whitcomb excursion train, Harry Wooley, pulled the No. 6 away from the station and onto the double tracks as instructed.[4] For some reason, however, instead of coming to a stop, Wooley continued onto the track on which the onrushing Pacific Express was traveling in the opposite direction. This single act set into motion a series of events that would have catastrophic consequences.

At that very moment, the Pacific Express No. 9, under the command of Engineer G. Cranshaw and Conductor John Bird, was less than a mile to the east. Three hours late, and heading westwards at a speed of forty miles per hour, a collision between the two trains was now unavoidable. After traveling just less than an eighth of a mile down the single track, the engineer of the No. 6 train spotted the oncoming light of the Pacific Express train just as it came around a slight curve that was hidden by the yard's telegraph office.

Almost simultaneously, the light of the Chicago & Grand Trunk Railway No. 6 also came into view of the Engineer Cranshaw of the Pacific Express train. Coming within sight of one another too late to prevent a collision, the engineers, and firemen of both trains placed their engines in reverse and engaged their brakes before jumping from their respective locomotives moments before impact.[5]

When the trains came together, the engine of the No. 6 train plowed nearly halfway through the locomotive of the Pacific Express, which was itself pushed into the baggage car. The terrific impact caused the first four coaches of the Pacific Express to telescope into one another.[6] Of these, the most severe devastation occurred when the third coach was forced into and over the second coach. When the third coach careened into the car ahead of it, the passengers in that coach were thrown violently forward with many coming to rest near the coach's wood stove.

As it was cold and rainy on that October evening, the stoves in the day coaches were in full use to provide some warmth for the passengers. Immediately following the accident, a blaze erupted in the mass of the No. 9's devastated coaches. Ignited by the oil lamps and wood burning stoves carried in these cars, the flames quickly spread, thus giving the survivors just seconds to make their escape.

All told, only ten individuals are known to have escaped the carnage visited upon the unlucky second coach, including one who was able to exit the car through one of its doorways. Meanwhile, the other survivors managed to escape the burning wreckage after smashing through windows on either side of the coach. This included three that exited the left side of the car, and at least six others that reached safety on the opposite side.[7]

Alerted by the sound of the crash, Henry Canfield, a Grand Trunk night clerk working in a nearby office, sounded the fire alarm and telephoned the engine house for assistance. Although the fire department arrived promptly on the scene, its efforts to control the blaze were hampered by the fact that the nearest hydrant was 2,000 feet away from the scene of the accident. Further complicating the rescue efforts was the difficulty experienced by the firefighters in maneuvering their hose wagon between the tracks and the wrecked railcars. These complications allowed the fire to gain a significant foothold before efforts to extinguish it could begin.

Not all those lucky enough to survive the shock of the collision were able to affect their escape before fire consumed the four wrecked day coaches. One of those was Mrs. Charles Van Dusen, of Fort Plain, New York. Despite having her legs

BURNING OF THE TELESCOPED CARS.

A contemporary newspaper illustration of the train collision at Battle Creek taken from the *Worth County Index*, dated October 26, 1893. (Author's Collection)

securely pinned in the wreckage, Mrs. Van Dusen somehow managed to get half of her body through a broken window. Responding to her cries for help, several people rushed over to her aid but were unable to free the unfortunate woman before the flames reached her.

The death of Mrs. Van Dusen made front-page news around the country. The following excerpt describing her fate, along with that of her husband, is one of the least graphic published and appeared in the October 20, 1893 edition of Syracuse, New York's *The Evening Herald*:

> The most horrible sight was that presented by Mrs. Charles Van Dusen of Fort Plain, N. Y. She succeeded in getting half way out of the window, but her legs were fastened, and those who ran to her assistance could not release her and she was burned to death before their eyes, with one-half of her body still hanging out of the window. Before death came to release her from her sufferings[,] she gave her name.
>
> The death of Mrs. Van Dusen was pathetic in the extreme. Her agony was terrible, but she retained her senses to the last, giving her name and address and telling those who were powerless to save her what friends to notify of her fate. She was a teacher in the Methodist Sunday school at home and she died like a Christian.
>
> Her husband, Charles Van Dusen, was terribly injured, but was taken from the wreck alive. He was removed to the Nichols Memorial home, where he died at 10 o'clock [October 20, 1893].

By the time that the firemen were able to put out the fire, the four wrecked coaches were little more than a pile of smoldering timber. Battle Creek's Nichols Hospital had just opened a few years previously, and it would be here that over 40 severely injured passengers would be taken. Even as the injured left the accident scene in carriages and carts, a gruesome search began for the dead in the twisted wreckage. Around 6 o'clock that morning, a little more than two hours after the accident, the first body was discovered by firemen picking through the debris. A few minutes later, a dozen more bodies were found clustered around the stove in the second coach. [8]

All told, twenty-six passengers from the Pacific Express No. 9 train were killed in the collision. After being removed from the wreckage, the dead were placed aboard a railcar that had been pressed into service as a temporary morgue. With many of the dead severely burned, it was virtually impossible to identify many of the victims by visual means. Therefore, some of the victims were subsequently identified by personal belongings found amongst their remains.

Suffering no injuries, the passengers traveling on the Raymond and Whitcomb excursion train fared far better than those aboard the Pacific Express No. 9. Besides the four coaches that burned, the collision also destroyed the steam locomotives from both trains. In fact, the engine belonging to the Pacific Express, known as No. 158, was a new Cooke locomotive that had been in use for only two weeks.[9]

Shortly after the accident, crews began clearing the wreckage from the track. The debris from the railcars was sorted and burned later that day, so that by the evening of October 20, 1893, the only thing remaining in the railroad yard from that morning's accident was a pile of ashes.[10]

Immediately following the wreck, Engineer Harry Wooley and Conductor Bertram Scott of the Raymond and Whitcomb special excursion train were arrested for their role in the accident. Concluding on November 14, 1893, the coroner's inquest into the wreck placed the blame for the wreck entirely upon Wooley and Scott. After hearing the relevant testimony, and deliberating for five hours, the jury at the inquest delivered the following verdict:

> "We find that the said collision was caused by gross disobedience of orders given by the train dispatcher. We also find that Conductor Bertram N. Scott and Engineer

Harry Woolley[*sic*] of train No. 6, eastbound, are guilty of
criminal neglect in running past their meeting point, at which
they had positive orders to stop."[11]

Immediately following the conclusion of the coroner's inquest,
the manslaughter trials of the two Grand Trunk employees
moved forward. It was decided that the trial of Conductor Scott
would proceed first, with its initial examination beginning on the
morning of November 15, 1893.[12] On December 26 of that year,
Bertram Scott was acquitted of the manslaughter charges
connected with the train collision. Newspaper stories at the time
reported that the trial for Engineer Wooley was scheduled to
begin in January of the following year. In light of the Conductor
Scott verdict, these same reports predicted that the prosecuting
attorney would drop the charges against the Grand Trunk
engineer. On January 17, 1894, this is exactly what took place as
the prosecutor entered a motion to drop all charges against
Engineer Wooley. This request was upheld by Justice Henry,
who dismissed the case.

# Chapter Four
## Detroit Water Tunnel Explosion - 1930

All cities require a source of freshwater for their citizens. Located on a connecting channel of the Great Lakes, Detroit was fortunate in having a plentiful supply of water as it grew into a major industrial center. Water pollution, however, was becoming a major problem by the early 1900s thus prompting the construction of the first water intake crib on the northern tip of Belle Isle in 1904. This structure would obtain water from Lake St. Clair that was free of near-shore pollution. As Detroit continued to grow in both size and population, additional water projects became necessary.

On the afternoon of Sunday June 8, 1930, workers were performing blasting operations in a water intake tunnel some 200 feet below the Detroit River. Stretching 8,200 feet in length, construction of the tunnel was nearing completion as it came within 200 feet of its destination on Belle Isle.[1] Out of the dynamite charges used that afternoon, at least three failed to detonate. These unexploded charges were left in place, thus setting into motion a sequence of events that would lead to deadly consequences.

The following day, as thirty men were working in the tunnel a sudden explosion occurred.[2] The blast killed four workers instantly, while two others later succumbed to their wounds. Killed in the explosion were James Harjer, Ellis Howe, Arthur Massey, Sam Sebolds, Pleas Tollison, and Charles Zuleski. All of the men killed ranged between the ages of 22 and 34 years old. Besides the fatalities, six other workers were seriously injured.

Some of the injured were taken to nearby St. Marys Hospital, while others went to Detroit Receiving Hospital for treatment.[3]

Taking place in a confined space, the explosion managed to knock all of the workers in the tunnel off their feet. Those nearest to the blast, and lucky enough to survive, were knocked senseless while sand and rock rained down upon them from the top of the tunnel. Despite being directly under the Detroit River, no appreciable amount of water entered the tunnel as a result of the explosion, with reports indicating that only a "few gallons" had seeped into excavation. Immediately following the blast, members of the fire and police departments cordoned off the area to keep the curious from interfering with the ongoing rescue operation.

After the dead and injured were located and all personnel were accounted for, four separate agencies began investigations into the accident. This included probes by the Detroit Police Department, the Prosecutor's Office, County Coroner, and the Mayor's Office. After receiving preliminary statements from tunnel employees and officials from the construction company responsible for building the tunnel, officials theorized that the explosion occurred when a worker's drill struck one of the unexploded dynamite charges left in the tunnel from Sunday's blasting operations.[4]

Within two days of the accident, press reports began appearing that quoted a Detroit Water Board official as laying the blame for the accident on Pleas Tollison, the day shift foreman whom had been killed in the blast. The following is an excerpt from an Associated Press report published in Benton Harbor's *The News-Palladium* on June 10, 1930:

> The blast was laid to a "piece of carelessness" by Torris Eide, tunnel engineer for the Detroit water board, who said that apparently a search was being made for an unexploded charge of dynamite.

> Eide said that Plas [sic] Tollison, day foreman, was careless in ordering so many men to work near the place where the dynamite was known to be. Tollison was one of those killed. All of the men in the immediate vicinity of the blast were killed or injured, and others more distant were stunned.

While appearing before a committee of investigators appointed by the mayor of Detroit, Charles Bowles, Torris Eide testified that 42 charges of dynamite were placed in the tunnel on the morning before the explosion. These charges would have amounted to approximately 430 pounds of explosives. After some of these failed to detonate as planned, this information was passed to the engineer in charge. While Tollison was in charge of searching for the unexploded charges, he was also responsible for keeping workers not engaged in the search out of the area. The engineer went on to testify to the board that Tollison had failed to do so as the handle and parts of a jackhammer were found at the spot of the explosion.[5]

Ironically, the day preceding the Detroit tunnel explosion, a similar accident occurred near Oakland, California when a blast tore through a tunnel under construction belonging to the Hetch Hetchy Water System. This accident killed seven workers and was caused when a gas pocket was opened during blasting operations, which remained undetected until the gas accumulated and detonated.

On December 11, 1971, some forty-one years following the 1930 tunnel accident, tragedy would once again strike a program designed to meet the water needs of the Detroit metropolitan area. During the construction of a major water project, 22 workers were killed following an explosion in a water tunnel that was under construction below the southern reaches of Lake Huron. While the 1930 explosion took place just north of downtown, near Belle Isle, the 1971 accident occurred some 70 miles north of the city. This blast was caused when a ventilation shaft being drilled by workers on the surface of the lake hit a methane gas pocket. A drill bit that fell into the shaft detonated the gas, which expended a large amount of energy into the tunnel below. After five years of construction, the Lake Huron Water Supply Project was completed in 1973 at a cost of $123 million.

# Chapter Five
## The Osceola Mine Disaster - 1895

In December 1836, the Michigan territorial government accepted a compromise brokered by the Federal Government to end a long-standing dispute with Ohio over the Toledo Strip. While the agreement greatly increased the proposed size of Michigan by granting it territory amounting to nearly three-quarters of the Upper Peninsula, many were unhappy with the arrangement as most of the new land gained was considered worthless. Following the conclusion of its territorial dispute with its southern neighbor, Michigan was granted statehood on January 26, 1837 as the 26th state.

The perceived worthlessness of the newly gained territory in the Upper Peninsula was to be short lived, however, as the discovery of sizable copper and iron deposits during the 1840s led to a mining boom in that part of the state. The copper deposits discovered in the area surrounding the Keweenaw Peninsula were unusual as they contained native copper, rather than the more common copper oxides and sulfides usually found in other copper producing regions. The extensive reserves of this valuable mineral led to the region becoming known as Copper Country, a name by which it is still commonly referred to despite the fact that mining continues only on a small scale.

During the late 1800s, it was possible to earn immense amounts of wealth in Copper Country as the following example illustrates. In May 1871, the Calumet and Hecla companies merged to become the Calumet & Hecla Mining Company. This firm was to produce over one-half of the copper mined in the United States between 1871 and 1880. As giants of Copper

Country, Calumet & Hecla made fortunes for its investors by having paid out $43,000,000 in dividends by September 1895. In fact, this firm had become so profitable that shareholders could anticipate the receipt of nearly $500,000 in dividends every 60 days.[1]

Located near the small village of Opechee, about 12 miles northeast of Houghton, the Osceola Consolidated Mining Company's Osceola Mine was located in the heart of Copper Country. Employing 500 workers, the Osceola Mine was a major employer in the area. Most of these employees were able-bodied men, but at least 40 young boys were on the payroll to perform light jobs on the surface and to carry drills for the men in the mines. Many of the workers lived in houses owned by the mining company, which while not considered as being extravagant nonetheless provided for a comfortable home.[2]

The previous two years leading up to 1895 had witnessed an economic downturn that had a drastic impact upon Michigan's mining industry. On the Gogebic Range, miners were desperate for work as the demand for iron plummeted, while in Marquette County iron miners were striking in hopes of securing better wages. Through this time, the Osceola mine continued to operate at a brisk pace with workers receiving wages at a slightly reduced rate compared to that paid during more prosperous times. In line with the other copper mines of the district, the workers at the Osceola Mine received wage increases during August 1895.[3]

Unlike many of the mining operations taking place in Michigan's Upper Peninsula, there was no friction between the workers and owners of the Osceola Mine. Despite the hazardous nature of the operation, the Osceola Mine had been considered as being very safe. This reputation would be shattered one early September morning during the waning years of the nineteenth century when the worst mining disaster to befall Copper Country took place.

On the morning of September 7, 1895, the day shift was busy with their chores when a fire was discovered at 11:30 a.m. in the Number 3 Shaft at the 27th level.[4] The shaft, which ran down at an angle of nearly 45 degrees, closely followed the vein of copper. The location at which the fire originated was roughly one-half mile below the surface and had been braced with a large number of cedar poles, or lagging as it was known to the miners, to prevent rock falling from the soft hanging wall.[5] When first discovered, the fire was considered a minor matter with Shift Boss Capt. Richard Trembath and a small group of men beginning efforts to extinguish it with buckets.

As the fire grew, a second captain, Richard Edwards, believing that a hose would be necessary to put water on the fire from a nearby water main, went to the surface. However, when Edwards attempted to reenter the mine after retrieving a hose, he found that the shaft had completely filled with dense smoke. Immediately thereafter, messengers were dispatched down the other shafts to pass word to the 200 men currently working below ground to evacuate.

As the alarm spread, many of the men in the mine were unconcerned about the fire as such occurrences were not uncommon in the mines. The assumption that there was only a small amount of wood present in the mine combined with previous experiences of underground fires being quickly extinguished gave many of the workers a false sense of security. There were many reports of men being warned of the fire and informed to evacuate which simply sat down and began eating lunch, preferring to go to the surface upon finishing their meal. In one instance, an older gentleman indicated that he always had a smoke after eating and would not begin heading to the surface until he had finished his pipe.[6] Such attitudes directly led to the high number of deaths at the Osceola Mine that Saturday afternoon as many could have survived had they heeded the fire warnings.

Regardless of their subsequent actions, all of the men in the mine, with the exception of the party actually fighting the fire, received warning of the blaze and were therefore given ample time to escape. As the fire intensified, Shaft No. 3 continued to fill with smoke and toxic gases. Men working in the mine were advised to go to the Opechee, the southernmost shaft, to affect their escape, as that shaft was clear of smoke.[7] To assist in helping the miners escape, mine skips in Shafts No. 4 and 5 remained in constant use. While many escaped by this method, others were able to exit the mine by climbing ladders.

As smoke billowed from Shaft Number 3, a crowd of onlookers began gathering around the mine. As word of the fire spread

As the fire continues below ground in Shaft # 3, smoke billows from its shaft house. (Michigan Technological University Archives and Copper Country Historical Collections)

throughout the local community, several family members of workers at the mine also began converging on the scene. Contemporary news reports indicate that the crowd around the mine eventually numbered in the thousands. After attempts to fight the fire were abandoned, and the last survivor had come to the surface, it was initially feared that up to 42 miners had failed to escape.[8] Later, this number was reduced to 30 following a more accurate accounting of mine employees was accomplished. The heavy smoke and gasses emitted by the fire prevented any attempt by rescue parties to enter the mine to conduct further searches for the missing.

After it became obvious that no hope remained of any additional survivors exiting the mine, the owners of the Osceola Mine made a final desperate effort to extinguish the blaze. In an effort to deprive the fire of oxygen, workers began sealing the opening to Shaft No. 3 at 4:30 in the afternoon. This was done by placing planks across the opening in the shaft house. Placed on top of the planks was a layer of sod and dirt, with each wisp of smoke penetrating the barrier receiving extra attention until every leak was plugged. Meanwhile, smoke began billowing out of Shafts No. 2 and 4, with each of these openings being likewise plugged. The sealing of these two shafts was somewhat easier as crews had less smoke to deal with than when sealing Shaft No. 3.[9]

On Monday morning, September 9, 1895, the opening to Shaft No. 4 was uncovered in response to appeals by those wishing to recover the dead. As it was believed that the victims were located between the twenty-seventh and tenth levels, it was hoped that the nearby No. 4 shaft would provide an access to these areas. An attempt to enter the shaft by a crew of searchers was quickly abandoned, however, as they were driven back by noxious gases and smoke. Following this, the decision was made Monday evening to once again seal the shaft.

Several additional attempts to search the mine took place during the early part of that week, all of which proved unsuccessful. It would not be until Thursday, September 12, 1895, that the shafts were ventilated sufficiently enough to allow searchers to descend into deeper levels of the mine. Twenty-three of the victims were discovered on the fourteenth level of the No. 4 shaft, while two more were located on the third level. The bodies of the remaining five missing miners were located in other parts of the mine.[10]

While performing their duties, rescue crews came across mute testimony concerning the last minutes of some of the miners killed. One of the victims, James Williams, had come agonizingly close to safety as he was found where he fell, only 300 feet from the surface. Searchers also discovered the body of the shift boss, Richard Trembath, on a ladder in the fourteenth

A group of onlookers poses for a photograph taken during the fire. (Michigan Technological University Archives and Copper Country Historical Collections)

level in a position that suggested that he was trying to take hold of a bell rope in an effort to signal the surface.

Besides Williams and Trembath, other victims included Richard Bickle, William Bryant, John Cudlip, Thomas Curtis, Walter Dahl, Alexander Daniel, William Donald, Richard Grenfell, James Harrington, Isaac Harrio, Barney Hellner, Robert Johns, Michael Johnson, Frank Lander, Jr., Peter Malmstrom, John Matson, Steve Oriski, Fred Peardon, Joseph Rasec, Steve Ristivick, Andrew Rosinski, Michael Schultz, Joseph Slotta, Michael Slotta, Peter Strandgaard, Veno Verbenz, Mike Voak, and Anton Zeswick.[11] Most of the men killed were experienced miners, with one reported as being sixty years in age. Among the dead, however, were four boys around the ages of 16 years old. As the majority of the miners had been married, the disaster left many children fatherless.

OSCEOLA MINE DISASTER.
(Scene at the Burning Shaft, in Whose Depths Thirty Miners Lost Their Lives.)

An illustration depicting the Osceola Mine fire published in the *Weekly Wisconsin* on September 21, 1895. (Author's Collection)

Another view of people gathering around the Osceola Mine on September 7, 1895. (Michigan Technological University Archives and Copper Country Historical Collections)

Captain James Richards, leader of the first search team into the shaft, along with other individuals associated with the mine were quoted nationwide in news reports stating that they believed the fire was the work of an incendiary. This led to a theory that someone had started the fire in an effort to cripple the mining company, a circumstance considered as being plausible. It was further theorized that such an individual could have believed that the miners could have easily escaped from the mine prior to any harm having come to them.[12] The possibility that the fire could have been intentionally set garnered much reporting in the press. The following excerpt is from the *Weekly Wisconsin*, dated September 21, 1895:

There are barely a half dozen places in the Osceola mine lagged up to keep out rock from dangerous places, but there was more lagging in this spot than elsewhere in the mine. If the mine was intentionally fired, it was in this spot that the incendiary would have touched his match, had he been well acquainted with the underground workings of the Osceola. That the fire was intentionally set seems too monstrous for belief but if accidental the deadly blaze could have been caused only by the most wanton negligence on the part of some passing miner, who threw a candle-butt or wick from his lamp upwards instead of downward, as most sane men would naturally do.

On September 12, 1895, a coroner's inquest into the disaster began at the Osceola Mine. During three days of testimony, Coroner MacDonald and Prosecuting Attorney Streeter questioned twelve witnesses in front of a jury. Deciding that every reasonable effort had been taken in spreading the fire alarm to the men in the shafts, and that the workers themselves contributed to their own deaths by not taking the evacuation order seriously, the jury exonerated the mine officials of any negligence in the disaster.[13]

It was determined that the lost miners fell into a fatal trap on the day of the fire by believing that Shaft No. 4, as a downcast shaft, would provide a safe avenue for escape. While this would have normally been the case, smoke and gas from the burning No. 3 shaft, which due to intense heat had changed from a downcast to an upcast shaft, was forced into the upper levels of the No. 4 shaft.[14] Therefore, the smoke and gas caught the miners as they were working their way to the surface, smothering them.

In the end, however, investigators could determine no apparent cause for the fire. The Mine Inspector's Report for Houghton County for 1895 stated that the origin of the fire would most likely remain a mystery, further adding that it most probably started from a candle or some snuff carelessly thrown by one of the men or boys working in the mine.

Following the fire, the Osceola Mine reopened, eventually being acquired by the Calumet & Hecla Mining Company in 1909. The mine remained active through 1931 when it was closed, only to reopen during the 1950s. In 1968, a labor strike caused the permanent shut down of both the Calumet & Hecla Mining Company and the Osceola Mine.

# Chapter Six
## Surviving the Great Storm - 1913

On November 7, 1913, what was to be the worst storm in terms of the number of steel vessels and lives lost was bearing down upon the Great Lakes. Known as the Big Storm of 1913 for generations, this weather system assaulted the freshwater seas for nearly four days. When the Storm finally abated, the level of devastation it had inflicted became clear with the realization that eleven ships and one barge, along with their entire crews, had been lost. Besides the sunken vessels, the storm also wrecked at least twenty-six other ships, several of which sustained damages severe enough that their owners declared them as total construction losses. Of the five Great Lakes, only Lake Ontario was fortunate not to have suffered any vessel losses during the great storm. By far, Lake Huron was the hardest hit with nine vessels wrecked upon its shores, while eight additional ships sailed to their doom in the expanses of the lake's storm tossed waters.

One of the few crews to survive the full fury of the 1913 Storm on Lake Huron belonged to the *Howard M. Hanna, Jr.*, which was owned by the Hanna Transit Company. Measuring 500 feet in length, this ship had been built in 1908 at Cleveland, Ohio by the American Ship Building Company. To operate their vessel, the Hanna Transit Company employed the W. C. Richardson & Company ship management firm based out of Cleveland.

When she entered service, the *Howard M. Hanna, Jr.* was typical of the new steel giants that entered service on the Great Lakes during the early twentieth century. As such, this ship was built to a design philosophy pioneered in 1869 by the steamer *R. J. Hackett*, which placed a ship's navigational equipment forward and the propulsion system aft. While such an arrangement allowed for a long and uninterrupted cargo hold that could be loaded and unloaded quickly by shore side equipment, it also afforded the crew the best possible vantage point to navigate their vessel. This was especially important while transiting narrow channels, which are common around the Great Lakes.

Steel lake freighters constructed during this timeframe represented a significant advancement in marine technology over the wooden steamers and schooners built during the late 1800s. As advanced as they were, however, ships such as the *Howard M. Hanna, Jr.* possessed one serious design flaw in that they were severely underpowered for their size. Powering the *Hanna, Jr.* was a 1,600 horsepower triple-expansion steam engine built by her builder's yard.[1]

On the morning of November 8, 1913, the *Howard M. Hanna, Jr.* departed Lorain, Ohio with 9,120 tons of soft coal destined for delivery to Fort William, Ontario.[2] Before departing the Ohio port, the steamer had also taken aboard 325 tons of coal to fuel her boilers. Commanding this 500-foot vessel as it slipped out of port that Saturday morning was Captain William Hagan.[3] Besides its captain, the *Hanna, Jr.* carried a crew that included twenty-three men and one woman.

As every Great Lakes mariner knows, the month of November demands unconditional respect for the brutality of its storms. When the *Howard M. Hanna, Jr.* began her voyage up the lakes, Captain Hagan took the necessary steps to ensure that his vessel was prepared to meet heavy weather. The coal loaded into the cargo hold was of a specific lower gravity than the primary commodity, iron ore, the steamer was designed to carry. Therefore, it was possible for crews working the coal loading equipment to fill the hold right up to the top of the hatch

The *Howard M. Hanna, Jr.* is shown during the early years of its operational career. (Author's Collection)

coamings without the risk of exceeding the ship's maximum draft. Loaded in such a manner, there was no possibility that the payload would shift in heavy seas.

After loading was completed, the deck crew began the arduous job of battening down each of the ship's fourteen hatches. To provide further protection against water entering the cargo hold, the hatches were fitted with heavy tarpaulins. Besides the attention given to securing the hatches, the deck crew also took care to lash down any movable objects on the exposed areas of the ship.

Throughout the balance of Saturday, the *Howard M. Hanna, Jr.* made her way across Lake Erie before entering the Detroit River to head northwards. In this river, she passed between the cities of Detroit and Windsor prior to proceeding past Belle Isle and into Lake St. Clair. After a journey of roughly twenty miles, the *Hanna, Jr.* threaded her way through the St. Clair Flats before entering the St. Clair River on Sunday morning. In this river the steamer continued her journey towards the upper lakes and by doing so passed several communities on the Michigan side that were home to a large number of Great Lakes sailors. In the order in which the *Howard M. Hanna, Jr.* passed them upbound, this included Algonac, Marine City, St. Clair, Marysville, and Port Huron.

After passing Port Huron, the *Howard M. Hanna, Jr.* entered into the lower reaches of Lake Huron, passing the Fort Gratiot Lightship at 5:12 a.m., November 9, 1913. As Captain Hagan would later recall, the weather at this time had continued to be fair and clear. This would change, however, as the ship passed Harbor Beach later that morning when the wind shifted for a few minutes to the southeast, before changing to the northeast and finally north-northeast. Following the last change in direction, the wind continued to increase in velocity.[4]

At 2:00 p.m., the *Howard M. Hanna, Jr.* passed Pointe aux Barques, near Port Austin, at a distance of five miles. Thus far on its voyage up the lake, the lumbering freighter had only experienced light snow, a circumstance that changed after 3:00 p.m. when heavy snow began blanketing the ship. While its 1,600 horsepower engine only allowed Captain Hagan's ship to make little headway against the steadily increasing strength of the winds, it was continuing to hold its own against the storm.

However, around 6:30 p.m., the *Howard M. Hanna, Jr.* began sustaining storm damage. First to be smashed by the waves was the oiler's door on the starboard side, which was closely followed by the loss of two engine room doors and windows. This allowed tons of cold lake water to enter the engine room. As the personnel in the engine room performed their duties in knee-deep water, the Chief Engineer, Frank Mayberry, remained in contact with Captain Hagan some 400 feet forward via telephone. Hagan, concerned about the engine, informed the

The *Howard M. Hanna, Jr.* aground near Port Austin after encountering the Storm of 1913. (Library of Congress)

chief engineer that he needed all the power they could get to keep the ship pointed into the wind.

At 7:30 p.m. the situation on the *Howard M. Hanna, Jr.* worsened when heavy seas crashed in the windows and doors to the engineer's room. Shortly after this, the cook's room and dining room were also ripped away with much of the woodwork and debris being deposited into the engine room. Accompanying this wreckage was the cook himself, Clarence Black, and his wife, Sadie.

While this was taking place, the forward crew, piloting the vessel, had lost sight of land in the heavy snow and were fighting desperately to keep the *Hanna, Jr.* pointed into the wind. Besides wrecking the after cabins, the waves also managed to knock in the windows and doors to the pilothouse. Meanwhile, the increasing severity of the storm prevented the crew of the ship to keep its bow pointed into the wind and it began to fall off course.

A short time before 10:00 p.m., the Port Austin Light was sighted, alerting the crew that the *Howard M. Hanna, Jr.* was coming dangerously close to the reef marked by that structure. Recognizing the danger, Captain Hagan ordered the first mate to drop the two bow anchors in an attempt to halt the steamer's drift. However, neither of the anchors managed to gain sufficient grip upon the lakebed and the helpless steamer was pushed broadside onto the reef at 10:00 p.m. that night.

The port side of the vessel struck the rocky bottom first, with additional wave action serving to push the *Hanna, Jr.* further upon the reef. This caused the ship to list to starboard as water rushed into the ship's hull, nearly reaching its main deck. Meanwhile, all of the hatches were ripped away by the relentless waves, with the stack being toppled onto the remains of the after cabins. When the *Howard M. Hanna, Jr.* finally came to rest she was about 900 feet away from the Port Austin Light.

Due to the weather conditions, the forward and after crews were isolated on opposite ends of the ship with no means for communication. Throughout Sunday night, Sadie Black managed to keep the after crew supplied with food and hot coffee despite working in waist deep water at times. The following afternoon, November 10, 1913, the third engineer managed to work his way forward with much appreciated food for crewmembers huddled together at the bow.

The morning following the stranding, distress rockets fired from the *Howard M. Hanna, Jr.* were spotted by Port Austin lifesaving crews. Unfortunately, they were hardly in a position to render immediate aid as the storm had buried their surfboat in the sand and severely damaged their boathouse and dock. Nonetheless, the lifesaving crew succeeded in launching a small lifeboat into the turbulent lake about one mile away from the station. About a half-mile off shore, however, the lifeboat filled with water, forcing the rescuers to beat a hasty retreat back to shore.

Following the failed effort to reach the *Howard M. Hanna, Jr.* in the lifeboat, lifesavers concentrated on extracting the surfboat from the sand. When it was finally retrieved, it was discovered to have several holes that required patching, a process that was not completed until late Monday night.

On Tuesday morning, the forward crew made its way aft to join the balance of the crew. While doing so, they noticed that a crack had developed in the hull of the *Howard M. Hanna, Jr.* near the number seven hatch.[5] With heavy seas still crashing into the hull, there was a danger that the ship could break up at any time. The crack, which was only about three inches wide when first discovered, would later increase to approximately eight inches by the time the crew left the ship.

A deck view of the devastated after cabins in which Sadie Black struggled to keep the crew fed. (Library of Congress)

Throughout all of this, Sadie Black continued to provide the crew with food and coffee as the seas threatened to tear the ship apart. Unsure as to whether or not their plight was known to those on shore, several crewmembers went out on deck Tuesday morning to remove the water and ice out that had accumulated in the sole remaining lifeboat, which was mounted on the port side of the ship. After lowering the lifeboat into the frigid waters, nine members of the crew began making their way to shore to summon help.

Unbeknownst to the men departing the *Howard M. Hanna, Jr.* the lifesaving crew was making a concurrent effort to reach the battered steamer. At 10:00 a.m., the two lifeboats met each other, with the lifesaving crew continuing to row towards the *Hanna Jr.*, where they took off seven of the ship's crew, including Sadie Black, on their first trip. At the time of their rescue, the crew feared that Mrs. Black could possibly die from exposure resulting from her many hours working in the cold water present in the galley.[6]

Although the lifesaving crew managed to bring the patched surfboat safely to shore, it leaked so badly that only constant bailing prevented it from sinking. After depositing the first group of survivors on land, the lifesavers immediately headed back to the *Howard M. Hanna, Jr.* to rescue the balance of the crew. This effort was successful, with the surfboat's crew erecting a sail to speed its return to shore.

In comparison to crews aboard the nine steamers that simply disappeared on Lake Huron during the 1913 Storm, the crew of the *Howard M. Hanna, Jr.* was extremely lucky, as all had managed to survive their ordeal. Following their rescue, several crewmen praised the actions of the only female aboard, Sadie Black, as can be seen in the following excerpt from the Associated Press that appeared in *The Waterloo Times-Tribune* on November 15, 1913:

*Milwaukee, Wis., Nov. 14.*-Mrs. Clarence Black, [street address omitted] Chicago, was the heroine of the wrecked steamer Howard M. Hanna, Jr., off Port Austin, Mich., Lake Huron, during the storm which swept over the great lakes, [*sic*] according to Arthur Jacobs, boatswain of the craft, upon his arrival here today.

Mrs. Black, the steward's wife, was the only cool one on the vessel after it went on the reef, Jacobs said. While all of the crew were huddled in the galley and mess room from Sunday night until Tuesday morning, Mrs. Black kept a fire going in the galley stove in spite of the water which was waist deep. She fed twenty five [*sic*] sailors and cheered them while the wind and waves were sweeping over the vessel and pounding it to pieces.

"When it came time for us to leave the ship and get into the life savers' boat, Mrs. Black refused the courtesies extended to a woman in the time of danger at sea," Jacobs said. "She took her turn in the order of her position and went over the side clad in the fireman's heavy shoes and with all the earmarks of a real sailor."

Sadie Black lost all of her clothes, jewelry, and $150 in cash, in the wreck. In recognition of her actions during the incident, the crew of the *Howard M. Hanna, Jr.* took up a collection for Mrs. Black following their safe arrival in Port Austin.[7] Acting upon a decision made prior to the 1913 Storm, Clarence and Sadie Black left working on the lake freighters following the wreck to begin a private business in Cleveland, Ohio.[8]

Deciding that the salvage of the stranded steamer was impractical, the owners of the *Howard M. Hanna, Jr.* abandoned her to the underwriters were she laid off Port Austin Light. The position of the vessel made for a difficult salvage job for which the insurance underwriters offered the Reid Wrecking Company 75% of the ship's value when she was released. Realizing that such an arrangement may be unprofitable given the ship's condition, Tom Reid made a counteroffer to purchase the vessel outright for $13,000. This offer was quickly accepted, and Reid

After being rebuilt, the *Howard M. Hanna, Jr.* was renamed the *Glenshee* and sailed the Great Lakes under the Canadian flag. (Author's Collection)

managed to pull the *Howard M. Hanna, Jr.* off its perch shortly thereafter.[9]

After being refloated, the wrecked ship was towed across Lake Huron to Collingwood, Ontario on the shores of Georgian Bay. Here the *Hanna, Jr.* was drydocked and given a survey, which confirmed that the ship could be rebuilt. Following its purchase by James Playfair for his Great Lakes Transportation Co., Ltd. fleet, it reentered service in 1915 under the Canadian flag as the *Glenshee*.[10]

In 1926, the *Glenshee* was acquired by the Canada Steamship Lines, and renamed *Marquette*. The following year, this 500-foot steamer was renamed *Goderich*. In 1963, this vessel was sold to one of the oldest fleets on the lakes, the Algoma Central Railway fleet. Following this transaction, the *Goderich* was renamed *Agawa* to honor both a railway station belonging to its owning company and a canyon located along its train route approximately 115 miles north of Sault Ste. Marie, Ontario.[11]

The *Agawa* continued to operate in the bulk trades upon the Great Lakes and the St. Lawrence Seaway until being surpassed by larger vessels. At the end of the 1967 shipping season, this ship laid up at Goderich, Ontario for the final time, its active career at an end. The *Agawa* was subsequently sold to serve as a grain storage barge at that port as the *Lionel Parsons*, a duty that lasted until 1983. During that year, the *Parsons* was towed out of Goderich bound for Lake Superior and Thunder Bay where it was cut up for scrap. As it left Lake Huron for the final time, those interested in the history of ships could reflect upon this vessel's long and active career following its near destruction upon those same waters some seventy years earlier.

# Chapter Seven
## A Name on a Tombstone

Sometimes, a link with the past can be discovered quite unexpectedly. Visitors to the McFadden Cemetery, located two miles northwest of Yale, in St. Clair County, will find a collection of grave markers dating from the mid to late 1800s. While not a large cemetery by any measure, it does however contain a gravestone with an intriguing inscription sure to spark the curiosity in anyone interested in history. This is the grave marker for William Bryce, whom passed away shortly following the end of the Civil War.

Although no battles took place on Michigan soil during the Civil War, the state was heavily involved in sending soldiers to fight in the Union Army. Of the 90,000 soldiers from Michigan to serve during the Civil War, some 14,000 would be killed. As is common with most wars fought throughout history, the historical record tends to concentrate upon figures belonging to the political and military leadership, while the primary participant, the average soldier, is all too often forgotten. Therefore, it was felt appropriate to add the story of William Bryce to this book, as although not representing a historical figure, he is part of our history nonetheless.

On May 10, 1835, a son was born to James and Elizabeth Bryce at Warwick, Ontario, whom they named William. James and Elizabeth Bryce had been married on May 21, 1834, in Adelaide, Canada. Shortly after his birth, William and his parents moved to Michigan, settling in St. Clair County. By 1860, William was working in Huron County as a laborer for a lumberman named Wesley Armstrong.

The era in which William Bryce grew up was one of the most tumultuous periods in the history of the United States. Opposing political and economic forces led to the eventual secession of eleven southern states from the Union beginning in December 1860 to form the Confederate States of America. This brought about the beginning of the Civil War on April 12, 1861 with the South's attack on Fort Sumter.

On May 13, 1861, at the age of twenty-six, William Bryce enlisted into Company G of the Third Michigan Infantry at Grand Rapids, Michigan.[1] Bryce mustered on June 10, 1861, and just three days later he and the rest of the regiment departed for Virginia. In March of the following year, Company G was transported by water from its winter encampment near Alexandria, Virginia to Fort Monroe on the southern tip of the Virginia Peninsula.

During the Second Battle of Bull Run, on August 29, 1862, William Bryce was wounded, later being hospitalized at the Presbyterian Church Hospital in Georgetown, Virginia. After spending over a month in the hospital, Bryce returned to his unit in October of that year. On December 24, 1863, William Bryce is recorded as having reenlisted at Brandy Station, Virginia with a rank of Corporal.[2]

On June 10, 1864, Corporal Bryce was transferred to Company F following the consolidation of the Third and Fifth Michigan Regiments. A few days later, on about June 15, 1864, William was wounded for a second time while his unit was engaged with the Confederate defenses emplaced around Petersburg, Virginia.

As winter approached during the second half of 1864, the Union forces engaged in the Richmond-Petersburg Campaign made an effort to seize the Boydton Plank Road. To accomplish this, Major General Winfield Scott Hancock ordered divisions from the II, V, and IX Union Corps and a cavalry division under the command of General David McMurtrie Gregg to withdraw

Following his capture at the Battle of Boydton Plank Road, William Bryce was taken to Richmond, Virginia, where he was held at the Libby Prison. (National Archives)

from the Petersburg lines to begin an offensive. Involving over 30,000 men, this was no minor movement of troops.

Following their withdrawal from the Petersburg lines, this force advanced to the west in an effort to cut off the Confederate supply lines by operating against the Boydton Plank Road and South Side Railroad. On October 27, 1864, the initial Union thrust succeeded in reaching one of the operation's primary objectives, the Boydton Plank Road. Whilst involved in this engagement, however, William Bryce was wounded for a third time and captured. Meanwhile, a counterattack by Confederate forces under the command of Major General Henry Heath succeeded in forcing a Union retreat from the Boydton Plank Road, which remained under southern control throughout the upcoming winter. Both sides suffered significant casualties in this battle with a combined 3,058 killed, of which the Union suffered the most heavily with 1,758 losses.[3]

Following his capture, Corporal Bryce was taken to Richmond, Virginia where he was imprisoned at the Libby Prison. During the Civil War, the harsh treatment of prisoners was commonplace with atrocities against their countrymen being committed by both sides. The Libby Prison, in particular, was notorious for the wretched conditions in which it held Union prisoners. Insufficient rations led to widespread malnutrition, while overcrowding aided the rampant spread of disease amongst the prisoner population. Originally built as a series of warehouses prior to its requisitioning by the Confederate Government in 1861, the prison was capable of holding approximately 1,200 prisoners, though at times this number was certainly exceeded.[4]

There is no known record of what William Bryce personally experienced while interned at the Libby Prison, although it must

A photograph taken in 2007 of William Bryce's tombstone in the McFadden Cemetery, which is located near Yale in St. Clair County. Over the years, an attempt has been made to restore the marker so that it can be read. (Author's Photo)

be assumed that he endured a hellish experience. On March 13, 1865, Bryce arrived at Camp Parole, near Annapolis, Maryland following being paroled earlier that month. Immediately afterwards, he was sent to Camp Chase near Columbus, Ohio. It appears that William Bryce spent little time at Camp Chase as he returned home to his family's farm in Brockway Township, Michigan sometime in late March.

Having been wounded on at least three separate occasions and compounded by his time spent in Libby Prison, the war had taken its toll on young Corporal Bryce. Suffering from dropsy, now better known as edema, William Bryce died on May 23, 1865 at the age of 30 years old and buried in the nearby McFadden Cemetery.

Belatedly, the Civil War had claimed yet another victim as William Bryce joined the estimated 620,000 Americans killed in that conflict. Following his burial, a tombstone was erected at the gravesite that left no doubt, as to what his family blamed on the untimely death of William Bryce. The inscription included the following quotation that has survived to this day:

> "His death was caused by starvation in one of the southern prisons."

# Chapter Eight
## Stove Capital of the World

Before becoming the automobile capital of the world, Detroit was known as the stove capital of the world. Blessed with its abundance of natural resources, Michigan was to become a major industrial center during the late 1800s. In 1865, one of the most important milestones in steel manufacturing took place at Wyandotte, when the Eureka Iron and Steel Company produced the first Bessemer process steel in the United States. While Michigan failed to become a major steel producing state, it nonetheless became home to a large number of industries producing products from iron and steel.

During the 1890s, Detroit became known for the manufacture of three major products, these being ships, railroad cars, and cast iron stoves. During this timeframe, the stove was beginning to replace the fireplace as the primary method to heat homes, with Detroit being home to the "Big Three" of stove producers, the Detroit Stove Works, Michigan Stove Company, and the Peninsular Stove Company. Besides these large companies, smaller firms such as Lansing's E. Bement and Sons and the Kalamazoo Stove Company also did their part in making Michigan a leader in the manufacture of stoves.

In 1861, Jeremiah and James Dwyer formed the firm of J. Dwyer & Company to begin manufacturing stoves in Detroit. Three years later, a stock company, of which William H. Tefft was the principal partner, acquired this foundry and renamed it the Detroit Stove Works. Originally incorporated with a capital of $50,000, the company grew quickly with its capitalization increasing first to $100,000 in 1865, and subsequently to

$300,000.[1]  The following excerpt describing operations at the Detroit Stove Works appeared in the August 3, 1871 edition of the *Grand Traverse Herald*:

> The largest force of men employed in any shop in this city is in that of the Detroit Stove Works Company, at Hamtramck. They are situated at an easy distance from the eastern terminus of the Jefferson ave. [*sic*] Street railway, on the edge, or rather down on the Detroit river [*sic*], having captured about 200 yards of the river by filling in.  The filling in and building with piers has been very great.  In the case of the stock shed, the earth has been raised from the bed of the river itself, and made into solid clay flooring, upon which rests, in store, tons of iron, coal, coke, and sand.  We see, from the stock shed, dockage with a very roomy slip for loading and unloading vessels, to the extent of 180 by 100 feet.

By 1890, the Detroit Stove Works was considered as being one of the largest industrial firms in the city of Detroit.  Located on Jefferson Avenue, the company employed 1,400 men and melted sixty tons of iron on a daily basis.  At this time, the company maintained a facility containing 325,010 square feet of space that included a warehouse along with separate foundry and mounting departments.  Extending to the shores of the Detroit River, the plant was ideally located to utilize waterborne transportation.  At the same time, the Detroit Stove Works was connected to all railroads entering the city by the Transit and Belt Line railways, with the former having a terminus in the company's yards.[2]

During 1890s, the Detroit Stove Works earned a reputation as being one of the best-equipped stove manufacturing establishments in the United States.  Of the products produced by this firm, the best known was its line of "Jewel" stoves and ranges.  Contemporary writing tells us that there were 800 different styles of "Jewel" stoves being produced by the Detroit

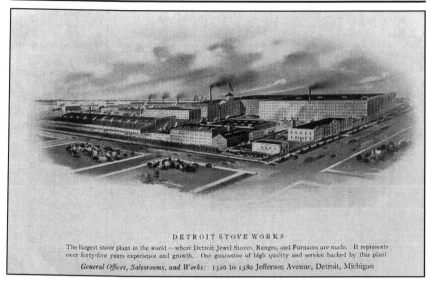

DETROIT STOVE WORKS

The largest stove plant in the world—where Detroit Jewel Stoves, Ranges, and Furnaces are made. It represents over forty-five years experience and growth. Our guarantee of high quality and service backed by this plant

*General Offices, Salesrooms, and Works:* 1320 to 1380 Jefferson Avenue, Detroit, Michigan

Artwork depicting the Detroit Stove Works plant, ca. 1910. (Library of Congress)

Stove Works during this period, with an annual volume of 60,000 units.[3] Furthermore, the "Jewel" line of stoves was remodeled on a yearly basis to meet the changing demands of their customers while incorporating the latest advancements in technology. As such, "Jewel" stoves and ranges were in demand the world over.

To meet the domestic demand for their products, the Detroit Stove Works opened branch offices in both Buffalo, New York and Chicago, Illinois. It also had numerous European agencies to market their stoves, including those in Vienna, Austria; Brussels, Belgium; Frankfurt, Germany; London, England; and Paris, France. The company also enjoyed a profitable export trade to Australia, South America, and Tasmania. By 1907, the Detroit Stove Works plant had grown in size to reach seven stories in height and covered an area in excess of fourteen acres.[4]

Representing a sizable investment for most customers, stoves are expected to incorporate a high degree of durability and reliability. During the early 1900s, the Detroit Stove Works went to great lengths marketing their stoves by proclaiming their use

# HAVE YOU A STOVE TO BUY?

*Foster Furniture Company inaugurates, Tuesday, Sept. 5, a great special sale for Fifteen Days of the Celebrated Jewel Stoves, of which they have the Exclusive Ft. Wayne agency*

The Jewel Stove Works is the largest stove plant in the World.

The works were established forty years ago, and more than four Million American homes are furnished with Jewel Stoves.

What this great concern does not know about making stoves nobody knows. Long experience has made Jewel stoves the best on earth.

And yet they cost no more than stoves of inferior quality.

You always win when you buy a Jewel, you generally lose when you don't.

Big Special Fall Sale at reduced prices for fifteen days of the entire line of Jewel cooking stoves, Jewel Steel Ranges, Jewel Oak Heaters, Jewel Hot Blast Stoves and the Celebrated Jewel Base Burners.

Not another such line can be found in Fort Wayne. *Sale Commences Tuesday, Sept. 5.* and will continue until Sept. 20 in order to accommodate those of our customers depending on the Railway pay-days.

## *Ten Per Cent. Discount For Stoves Paid For Before Delivery, Five Per Cent. Discount To Our Credit Customers*

| Opening Begins Tuesday, Sept. 5th | Our entire line of Jewel Stoves has arrived and been placed on sale. It constitutes by all odds the greatest assortment of stoves ever placed before the Fort Wayne public. To cause early buyers of these world-wide famous stoves, we will make a special sale upon them for the next fifteen days, giving you the same prices that we usually give you at our closing out sales late in the winter. | Sale Ends Wednesday Sept. 20th |
| --- | --- | --- |

### Note This Liberal Inducement

Select the stove you want from our big stock, pay us a small amount as evidence of good faith that you will take the stove, and we will deliver it any time you say previous to November 1st. Stoves bought on this plan will be sold at the same prices as those immediately delivered, so do not hesitate to take advantage of the sale prices we offer and get your stove while you have the opportunity to select from an assortment that has not been picked over.

### Remember We Sell You Genuine

## BUY A JEWEL AND SAVE FUEL

# Jewel Stoves

Which are the very best that money can buy. For over forty years Jewel Stoves have been recognized as the leading Stoves Manufactured by the Largest Stove Plant in the World. They are made to last and save fuel as over 4,000,000 buyers can testify. Our stock comprises the leading Jewel styles in Base Burners, Steel Ranges and Heaters.

Large Stoves, Good Stoves, Stoves which will last a lifetime, cost a considerable amount of money, but by buying now and paying $5 or $10 a month upon one, you will have it pretty well paid for before the coal bills come in. We will keep it for you until you are ready for it, and if you buy within the next 15 days and it is all paid for when delivered, you shall have 10 per cent. off from our lowest cash prices, and if you want it charged you may have it delivered now, or at any time, and still receive 5 per cent. discount from our best cash prices.

**REMEMBER, SALE COMMENCED AT 8 A. M., TUESDAY, SEPTEMBER 5.**

An advertisement appearing in the *Fort Wayne Daily News* on September 4, 1911 announcing a sale on the Detroit Stove Works' line of Jewel stoves. (Author's Collection) of a special mixture of stove plate known as Kemi-test metal. This material was said to make stoves that were tough and long lasting. Company brochures distributed in 1907 relate that there were over 4,000,000 "Jewel" stoves and ranges in use throughout the United States alone.

By 1920, the Detroit Stove Works was continuing to grow with W. T. Barbour as its president and J. A. Fry serving as general manager. In 1923, the company acquired the Art Stove Company, this being followed in 1925 by the acquisition of one of the former "Big Three" stove makers of the 1890s, the Michigan Stove Company. Following this transaction, the combined enterprise was renamed the Detroit-Michigan Stove Company.

In 1871, Jeremiah Dwyer left the Detroit Stove Works to form the Michigan Stove Company.[5] This company, which also resided on Jefferson Avenue, marketed its stoves and ranges exclusively under the "Garland" product line. By 1891, the Michigan Stove Company was building between 250 and 300 stoves per day, with some 60,000 to 70,000 units produced annually. During this same time period, the company reportedly paid out approximately $40,000 in monthly wages to its employees, the level of which averaged between 1,000 and 1,200 workers.[6]

Besides obtaining iron from the mines located in the Lake Superior region to produce their products, the Michigan Stove Company also received iron shipments from Hanging Rock, Ohio; Chattanooga, Tennessee; and Birmingham, Alabama. In the foundry, workers combined aluminum with iron to produce the base material for the production of "Garland" stoves.[7] Such a combination produced smooth castings, prevented cracking, and incorporated additional strength compared to regular cast iron.

As was the case with the Detroit Stove Works, the Michigan Stove Company became world renowned for the quality of its

61

products. By 1891, the company had opened large branch houses for the sale of "Garland" stoves and ranges in Buffalo, Chicago, New York City, and a number of foreign cities.

In 1881, James Dwyer formed the Peninsular Stove Company, thereby creating the final member of Detroit's "Big Three" stove makers. While many of Michigan's stove makers were based in Detroit, the industry was by no means confined to the city. By 1900, there were twenty-one firms in the state producing stoves, thirteen of which were located outside the city of Detroit. [8]

In 1926, the newly combined Detroit Stove Works and Michigan Stove Company, the Detroit-Michigan Stove Company, posted one of its best financial years with net sales amounting to $8.1 million and net profits of $1.2 million. Such performance, however, was not to last after August 1929 with the onset of the Great Depression. During the 1930s, annual sales fell as low as $2.3 million per year, with the Detroit-Michigan Stove Company

A photograph of the Michigan Stove Company, with the gigantic Garland Stove displayed on its grounds, ca. 1915-1925. (Library of Congress)

losing money for each year between 1931 and 1934. By 1940, however, the company was profitable once again, with the posting of a net profit of $210,000 that year on net sales equaling $3.1 million.

In 1945, the Detroit-Michigan Stove Company acquired A-B Stoves, Incorporated of Battle Creek. During this timeframe the company also expanded by adding a metal fabricating division which produced automotive parts. During 1948, this company was reporting an annual profit of nearly $2 million on net sales of $21 million. Fortunes for the Detroit-Michigan Stove Company were to change in 1949, however, when sales declined by nearly half, a downturn from which it would never fully recover.

After experiencing several years of poor performance, the Detroit-Michigan Stove Company was acquired by Welbilt Stove in 1955. Following this acquisition, the consolidated company became the Welbilt Corporation. In 1957, the Detroit plant was shuttered, thus bringing to an end a chapter in the city's manufacturing history.

After the plant closure, however, there remained one enduring symbol of Detroit's once proud status as stove capital of the world. In 1893, the Michigan Stove Company constructed a large "Garland" stove replica for display at the Chicago World's Fair, which opened in May of that year. Constructed primarily of wood and weighing nearly 15 tons, the stove stood 25 feet high, 30 feet long, and 20 feet wide. Following the conclusion of this event, the stove was transported to Detroit where it was reassembled and placed alongside Michigan Stove's plant on East Jefferson Avenue.

Following the merger of the Michigan Stove Company and the Detroit Stove Works in 1926, the giant stove was refurbished and moved next to the headquarters of the newly formed Detroit-Michigan Stove Company at intersection of Jefferson and East Grand Boulevard, near the Belle Isle Bridge.[9] Here the mammoth

*GARLAND STOVE CO.'S EXHIBIT AT THE WORLD'S FAIR*

An 1893 newspaper illustration of the giant Garland Stove. (Author's Collection)

stove stood until it was moved to the Michigan State Fairgrounds in 1965.

In a deteriorated condition, the stove replica was disassembled during 1974, and placed in storage at the Fort Wayne Military Museum. Here it quietly languished until 1998, when efforts to restore the stove proved successful. Restored to its original appearance, the newly rebuilt stove was unveiled on August 24, 1998, just prior to the grand opening of the Michigan State Fair. Sadly, just less than thirteen years later, on August 13, 2011, the giant "Garland" stove was destroyed by fire. The blaze, which was blamed on a lightning strike, completely destroyed the upper works of the stove, leaving only the pedestal standing. Thus, one of the last remaining symbols of a bygone industrial era in both the history of Detroit and Michigan was lost.

# Chapter Nine
## The Struggle to Join Two Peninsulas

Today, most people living in Michigan cannot recall a time before the Mackinac Bridge connected the state's two peninsulas. This bridge, which opened to traffic on November 1, 1957, remains an engineering marvel and has become one of the most important structures in the state. While construction of the Mackinac Bridge began on May 7, 1954, the actual story concerning efforts to span the Straits of Mackinac begins some seventy years earlier. As the building of the Mackinac Bridge is worthy of a work dedicated to the subject, the events leading up to its construction will be the focus of this chapter.

Granted statehood in 1837, Michigan became the only state in the union consisting of two peninsulas. Dividing these two landmasses is the Straits of Mackinac, which measures just less than four miles at its narrowest width. Throughout early history, this waterway formed a barrier to traffic heading north and south between Michigan's peninsulas. Native American tribes that spoke the Algonquin language dominated this region of Michigan. This included the Chippewa or Ojibwa that generally lived north of the Straits, and the Ottawa that resided to the south. It was from these people that the area was given the name Michilimackinac, or great road of departure.[1] Such a meaning was quite fitting as the Straits caused traffic in the area to concentrate upon an east-west pattern.

In September 1634, the French explorer Jean Nicolet became the first European to enter the Straits of Mackinac. Assigned a mission to venture further west than any other explorer up to that time, Nicolet was searching for a passage to China. As

Nicolet ventured west from the Straits of Mackinac, however, he was confronted not by an ocean of saltwater, but another large expanse of freshwater that would later become known as Lake Michigan.

In 1671, the French established the first permanent European presence in the Straits of Mackinac when Jacques Marquette built a Jesuit mission on the northern side of the Straits at what is now known as St. Ignace.[2] This followed Marquette's founding in 1668 of a mission at Sault Ste. Marie, which was the first European settlement in Michigan. To defend their territory, the French established Fort de Buade at St. Ignace in 1690.

In 1698, the French reduced their military presence in the Straits by abandoning Fort de Buade. However, an expansion of British influence into the upper Great Lakes region prompted a return of French forces in 1715 with the establishment of Fort Michilimackinac. This fortress was built on the southern side of the Straits at what is present day Mackinaw City. In 1761, following the conclusion of the French and Indian War, France ceded Fort Michilimackinac to Britain, which maintained it as a trading post. In 1763, during Pontiac's Rebellion, Native Americans captured the fort and killed a majority of its British occupants.

The British recaptured Fort Michilimackinac in 1764, but later relocated their forces to a fortress built on Mackinac Island in fear of an attack by American colonists. The Straits remained under British control until 1796, when it, along with the territory that would later become Michigan, was transferred to the United States. Throughout this time period, the vital waterway remained the center of the northwest fur trade.

In 1805, Michigan became a territory with its Upper Peninsula consisting of an area roughly one-half of its present size. At the time, the northern reaches of the territory were largely unknown, with a concerted effort to explore this region not beginning until after the War of 1812. By 1833, the Michigan Territory had grown to encompass an area that would eventually become the states of Wisconsin, Minnesota, Iowa, and the eastern portions of North and South Dakota. In July 1836, the western portion of the Michigan Territory was divided to become the Wisconsin Territory in preparation of Michigan achieving statehood. While the original boundaries of this division only granted Michigan approximately one-third of the Upper Peninsula, the border was subsequently moved further west to its present location in compensation for Michigan abandoning its claim on the Toledo Strip in December 1836.

On January 27, 1837, President Andrew Jackson signed legislation allowing Michigan to become the twenty-sixth state. Meanwhile, the Straits of Mackinac continued to act as a boundary between residents living in the Upper and Lower Peninsulas. Such a disconnection served to create separate economic and political agendas for the populations of the two peninsulas. It also led to a cultural divide between these two

The railroad car ferry *Sainte Marie*, built in 1893, transits the Straits of Mackinac on its regular route between St. Ignace and Mackinaw City, ca. 1900. (Library of Congress)

groups, causing Michigan to resemble two separate states rather than a single political entity. These moods were further fostered by the fact that it was often easier for those living in the Upper Peninsula at the time to travel to Milwaukee or Chicago than it was to travel to Lansing or Detroit.[3]

While the Straits of Mackinac formed a formidable obstacle to widespread commerce between the two peninsulas, traffic across this waterway had existed since the earliest days of history, albeit on a small scale. Initially, this consisted of the occasional Indian paddling a canoe across the Straits. Later, the British employed barges to supply their fort on Mackinac Island. During the winter months, the Straits froze over, and by doing so provided an avenue for a somewhat hazardous journey between the two peninsulas by foot, horseback and even dog team.[4]

While expansion of the railroads during the later part of the nineteenth century would play a major role in the economic growth of Michigan, it did little in alleviating the isolation of the state's two peninsulas. In 1880, the only direct rail link to the Upper Peninsula was through Chicago, and while vessel traffic on the lakes enabled trade between Upper and Lower Michigan, such commerce was limited to the months of the navigational season.

This was to change in 1881 when three railroad companies, one at St. Ignace and two at Mackinaw City, formed a subsidiary, the Mackinac Transportation Company. To convey freight across the Straits of Mackinac, this company purchased the break-bulk steamer *Algomah*. Crews would load this vessel by hand with cargoes from railcars at St. Ignace or Mackinaw City, which would in turn be reloaded into railcars on the opposite side of the Straits. However, as a large percentage of the cargo shipped through this rail connection consisted of copper either in barrels or in the form of ingots, such an operation proved difficult. In an attempt to address this deficiency, the Mackinac Transportation

Company purchased a barge, named *Betsy*, to carry railcars while being towed behind the *Algomah*.[5] While this initial attempt at creating a rail link between the Upper and Lower Peninsulas had numerous limitations, it nonetheless proved that such an operation was feasible. This led to the construction of the purpose-built wooden railroad car ferry *St. Ignace* by the Detroit Dry Dock Company in 1888.

Over the next 25 years, the Mackinac Transportation Company built three additional car ferries to operate in the Straits of Mackinac. Intended to operate year-round in harsh conditions, these vessels were often employed as icebreakers when the need arose. The maintaining of a rail link between Michigan's Upper and Lower Peninsulas continued for just over 100 years, before the last railroad ferry operating in the Straits, the *Chief Wawatam*, was idled in August 1984.

A copy of William Saulson's 1884 newspaper advertisement using the newly opened Brooklyn Bridge to advocate a similar span across the Straits of Mackinac. (Author's Collection)

Around the same time that a rail connection across the Straits of Mackinac was being established, there began some interest in developing a bridge to span the waterway. By 1884, several articles began appearing in area newspapers, including the *Grand Traverse Herald*, advocating the bridging of the Straits. The encouragement to build such a span can be attributed in some part to the opening of the Brooklyn Bridge at New York City on May 24, 1883. In fact, William Saulson, a merchant with stores in St. Ignace and Seney, published several newspaper advertisements during 1884 portraying the Brooklyn Bridge with the following caption: "A Glimpse of the Future...The Proposed Bridge across the Straits of Mackinac."[6] Saulson also used this image, made from a woodcut he had acquired, to adorn wrapping paper used by his shops.

The growing tourist industry in the Straits of Mackinac area during the 1880s played a significant role in ambitions to build a bridge. A major proponent of such a project was Cornelius Vanderbilt II, chairman of the Mackinac Island Hotel Company that had built the Grand Hotel on Mackinac Island in 1887. Speaking before a meeting of the company's directors on July 1, 1888, Vanderbilt had the following to say:

> "We now have the largest well-equipped hotel of its kind in the world for a short season business. Now what we need is a bridge across the straits [*sic*]."[7]

Vanderbilt's comments came at a time in which the United States was becoming heavily industrialized, thereby bringing about an era of optimism in which such engineering projects began to appear practical. While it was realized that the economic potential of Michigan's Upper Peninsula would never be fully realized without a permanent link with the Lower Peninsula, it would not be until the use of the automobile became widespread that interest in a bridge across the Straits would be rekindled.

The early 1920s saw two proposals to connect Michigan's peninsulas by road. The first of these was proposed in 1920 by Horatio "Good Roads" Earle, Michigan's first state highway commissioner, which called for the construction of a floating tunnel to span the Straits.[8] The following year, Charles Evans Fowler, an engineer from New York, suggested the building of a series of causeways and bridges to span the Straits. Using Cheboygan as a starting point, this plan envisioned first connecting the Lower Peninsula to Bois Blanc Island. From there, the route would continue to both Round and Mackinac Islands before terminating at St. Ignace.[9] While Fowler's plan seemed more practical than the floating tunnel concept championed by Horatio Earle, it suffered the same fate as neither proposal was acted upon.

By the early 1920s, automobile and passenger traffic across the Straits of Mackinac had increased to the point that the railroad car ferries could no longer meet the demand. Responding to this situation, the Michigan Legislature ordered the State Highway Department during 1923 to begin operating a ferry service between the Upper and Lower Peninsulas. This service began on July 31 of that year, when the ferry *Ariel* entered service. This diminutive 95-foot wooden steamer had previously been engaged in transporting passengers across the Detroit River. To prepare the *Ariel* for the hardships it would face in the Straits of Mackinac, the State Highway Department had its hull sheathed with iron.[10] With a capacity of only twenty vehicles, however, the *Ariel*'s career with the State Highway Department would only last a few seasons before it was sold following the arrival of larger vessels.

The beginning of a dedicated ferry service across the Straits did much to boost commerce between Michigan's peninsulas. The following excerpt describing the growth of cross-Straits travel during 1923 appeared in *The Ironwood Times* on February 15, 1924:

> Conclusive evidence relative to the remarkable increase in the tourist traffic over the Straits of Mackinac during the past year is contained in two reports recently received by the Upper Peninsula Development Bureau. These reports were issued by the State Highway Department, operating the car ferry Ariel, and by the Michigan Central Railway and D. SS. & A. Railway, operating the ferry Waw-Waw-Tam [Chief Wawatam].
>
> The report of the state highway department shows that from July 31 to November 19, the period during which the highway department's ferry was in operation last year, 10,379 cars were ferried across the Straits of Mackinac, including the traffic both north and south. This includes also the passengers carried in each car, and the reports sets forth, further, that 2,418 passengers in addition to those carried in the cars crossed the Straits of Mackinac on the ferry during 1923. The total revenue derived from this source given as $28,432,500.

The same newspaper article goes on to report that the railroad car ferry *Chief Wawatam* carried an additional 9,432 automobiles across the Straits during that same year. When combined with the figure given for the State Highway ferry that year, it can be ascertained that 19,811 vehicles made the journey between the Upper and Lower Peninsula during 1923. Considering that only 10,000 automobiles made such a transit during 1922, traffic across the Straits had increased at a phenomenal rate.[11]

The growth experienced in the number of automobiles making their way back and forth across the Straits in 1923 was pale in comparison to those carried in 1924. During that year, some 38,000 vehicles were transported between Mackinaw City and St. Ignace. In just two years of operation, the State Highway's ferry system had permitted automobile traffic between Upper and Lower Michigan to nearly quadruple.

In 1928, realizing that a system of ferries would be unable to sustain such a rate of growth, Governor Fred W. Green instructed the Highway Department to conduct a feasibility study concerning the construction of a bridge across the Straits of Mackinac.[12] While the report for this survey concluded that such a bridge was feasible, the cost of its construction would amount to $30,000,000. With such a staggering cost, little progress was made towards the building of a cross-Straits bridge during the late 1920s and early 1930s.

Ironically, the Great Depression offered the possibility of such a project receiving federal public works funding. In 1934, the Michigan State Legislature created the Mackinac Straits Bridge Authority in an effort to secure such funds. This organization was tasked with developing engineering concepts, issue bonds to cover its cost, build the bridge, and finally to operate it. In 1935, the Bridge Authority presented a proposal to the federal government based upon Charles Fowler's island-hopping concept from 1921. After being rejected, a follow up proposal calling for a single span connecting Mackinaw City and St. Ignace was submitted in September of the following year, which was also denied federal funding.

Despite the lack of any backing by the federal government, the Mackinac Straits Bridge Authority continued to pursue the construction of a bridge. In 1937, the Authority retained one of the foremost bridge engineering concerns in the world when it contracted the firm of Modjeski and Masters to provide a construction report pertaining to a cross-Straits bridge.[13] During this time, soundings and borings were made to produce a geological study of the bridge's intended path across the Straits of Mackinac.

While the subject of connecting Michigan's two peninsulas with a bridge created considerable debate between proponents and opponents alike, it also stirred the imagination. There was also a feeling among many that the true economic value of the Upper Peninsula was constrained only by the ferry system operating on the Straits. The following excerpts reflect a common theme appearing in newspapers during this time, and were taken from an article published in *The Sheboygan Press* on June 29, 1937, which had originally appeared in the *Escanaba Daily Press*:

> Ten ferry boats will not be able to handle the tourist rush at the Straits of Mackinac in the not distant future. Prof. Cissel of the University of Michigan declared in an address at the meeting of the Upper Peninsula Development bureau [*sic*].
>
> There is no denying that the traffic at the Straits of Mackinac is steadily increasing each year. This year, the state highway department [*sic*] will have five boats in the service. As the ferry boat service is improved, more tourists seem to come up into this north country.

While also relating the opinion of those opposed to building a bridge across the Straits, it quickly becomes apparent that this article was written in favor of such a project as the opposing viewpoint is quickly tempered by the use of a comparison with history obviously intended to discredit skeptics:

> The practical-minded folks are still pooh-poohing the Straits of Mackinac bridge proposal and are insisting that the ferry boat service always will be able to take care of the transportation needs between the two peninsulas. They claim that the traffic will never be heavy enough to warrant the construction and maintenance cost of a huge span across the [S]traits. Perhaps, we should give encouragement, however, to those men, who have the courage to dream of gigantic engineering projects. These visionary men should be commended for their persistency in the face of criticism. In an early day, practical folks scoffed at Robert Fulton. Who knows, but that maybe these Straits of Mackinac bridge proponents will have the last hearty laugh someday.

One of the recommendations put forth in the engineering report generated by Modjeski and Masters called for the construction of 4,200-foot causeway into the Straits from St. Ignace. In August 1940, Murray D. Van Wagoner, state highway commissioner, and future governor, asked the state administrative board to authorize the construction of this causeway. Besides being a stepping-stone towards the eventual building of a span across the Straits, it was intended that the causeway would also serve as a ferry dock pending the construction of a bridge. This would effectively reduce the distance traveled by the ferries on each trip from nine miles to just three, while at the same time avoiding two shoals.[14]

Had global events not intervened it is entirely reasonable that construction of a bridge across the Straits of Mackinac would have began sometime during the 1940s. The outbreak of the Second World War, however, placed enormous demands on the nation's resources, and it soon became apparent that it would be necessary to delay such a project as the following excerpt appearing in *The Ludington Daily News* on January 25, 1941 relates:

> Prof. James H. Cissel, former secretary of the Mackinac Straits Bridge [A]uthority, said today that plans to link Michigan's two peninsulas with [a] huge suspension bridge should be delayed because of national defense demands on structural material.
>
> Prof. Cissel, University of Michigan authority on bridge design, contended that neither the volume of steel nor a huge federal expenditure for the project should be made available at the present time.

While the shortage of steel brought upon by the war would delay the construction of a bridge span, it did not prevent the causeway project from proceeding. On August 5, 1941, State Highway Commissioner G. Donald Kennedy, with the approval of Governor Van Wagoner and a team of engineering experts, announced that bids were to be accepted later that month for the construction of the causeway extending into the Straits from the north shore.[15] The contract for the causeway was awarded on September 30, 1941.[16]

Work on the causeway began in October 1941, with workers descending onto the 245-acre site that month.[17] Stone and gravel for the project was easily obtained from local quarries and transported to the site by truck, rail, and water. Work continued through the balance of 1941 until being stopped by the onset of winter. By August of 1942, newspapers were reporting the $616,000 causeway was forty percent completed, with Commissioner Kennedy being quoted as estimating the first phase of the project would be completed during October of that year. At the time, it was still envisioned that the causeway would be equipped with landing facilities to serve as a ferry terminal under a separate contract.

Weather conditions in the Straits of Mackinac can be among the worst experienced throughout the entire Great Lakes region. During September 1943, high waves managed to inflict serious enough damage to the causeway to prompt State Highway Commissioner Charles M. Ziegler to pay a personal visit to St. Ignace to survey the damage.[18]

Commissioner Ziegler opposed the construction of a bridge over the Straits of Mackinac as is related in the following paragraph taken from an article appearing in Benton Harbor's *News-Palladium* on October 14, 1943, discussing Upper Michigan's work plans following the war:

> At a smaller conference of planning officials last month at Higgins Lake[,] state highway Commissioner Charles M. Ziegler indicated he looked with disfavor on the bridge idea, developed by his predecessors.

A postcard view of the automobile ferry *Vacationland*, which became the last such vessel built for service on the Straits of Mackinac. (Author's Collection)

Following the end of the war, support for a Mackinac Straits bridge faded somewhat, leading to the Michigan Legislature abolishing the Mackinac Straits Bridge Authority in 1947. Shortly afterwards, a contract was awarded to the Great Lakes Engineering Works at Ecorse, Michigan for the construction of a new auto ferry capable of year-round operation on the Straits of Mackinac. Named *Vacationland*, this double-ended ferry cost $4,745,000 and was the largest such ship in the world when it entered service on January 15, 1952.

Although the *Vacationland*, and its capability of carrying 150 vehicles, increased the State Highway's fleet of five ferries overall single-trip capacity to 500 automobiles, travelers between the peninsulas could still expect significant delays. During certain times of the year, such as tourist and hunting seasons, it was not uncommon for drivers to experience delays of up to five hours.

By 1950, proponents for a bridge to replace the car ferry operation had gained enough support to compel the State Legislature to create a new Mackinac Bridge Authority. On June 6, 1950, the newly appointed members of the Authority took office, including its chairman Prentiss M. Brown, whom had been a longtime supporter of a Mackinac Straits bridge.[19]

In January of 1951, the Mackinac Bridge Authority issued an engineering report stating that construction of a bridge would cost $86,000,000. However, because of a shortage of steel due to the Korean War, legislation to finance construction was delayed until 1952. On April 30 of that year, the Michigan Legislature approved the building and financing of the bridge. Following the sale of $99,800,000 worth of bonds during late 1953, the Mackinac Bridge Authority received a certified check for $96,400,033.33 on February 17, 1954.[20] With the funds finally available to finance a Mackinac Straits bridge, contracts for its construction were promptly awarded.

On May 7, 1954, some seventy years after William Saulson had first published his advertisements promoting a suspension bridge across the Straits of Mackinac, actual construction began. Designed by Dr. David B. Steinman, the Mackinac Bridge was the most expensive suspension bridge built in the world when it was opened to traffic on November 1, 1957, costing more than the Golden Gate and George Washington Bridges combined. While developing the bridge, Dr. Steinman incorporated the causeway built at St. Ignace during the 1940s into his design, thus saving some $3,000,000 in construction costs.[21]

While the Mackinac Bridge was under construction, cross-Straits traffic reached new heights. During 1955, the Highway Department's fleet of ferries carried over 900,000 vehicles, a number that would be exceeded during the first ten months of 1957 alone. Following the opening of the Mackinac Bridge, the

The completed Mackinac Bridge as viewed from St. Ignace during the 1960s. The causeway, built during the 1940s on the north side of the Straits of Mackinac, is at the extreme left of this picture. (Library of Congress)

auto ferry service across the Straits became redundant and was promptly abandoned.

By creating a physical link between its two peninsulas, the Mackinac Bridge opened up a new chapter in Michigan's history by conquering a natural barrier to its continued economic and cultural growth. Today just over 3.7 million vehicles pass over the Straits of Mackinac each year, a number that would have been impossible without the building of the Mackinac Bridge.[22]

# Chapter Ten
## Michigan's Oldest Lighthouse

Bordered by four of the five Great Lakes, it is not surprising that Michigan has a rich maritime history. The commerce traveling on these waters played a significant role in the state developing into a major industrial center by the early 1900s. The lakes themselves, however, can be extremely hazardous bodies of water. In fact, the first ship to sail on the upper Great Lakes, La Salle's *Le Griffon*, disappeared in 1679 on the return leg of its maiden voyage.[1]

By the 1820s, shipping had grown to such a level that the government recognized the need to make navigational improvements to the Great Lakes. One of these was the requirement for a beacon at the southern tip of Lake Huron where the lake flows into the St. Clair River. On March 3, 1823, Congress appropriated $3,500 to build a lighthouse near Fort Gratiot, which would become the first such structure built in the Michigan Territory.

With funds allocated, a construction contract for the Fort Gratiot Light was awarded to Winslow Lewis, a Massachusetts contractor that was to build many lighthouses around the United States during the early 1800s. Lewis was also the inventor of the Lewis lamp, which was used as a standard source of illumination in lighthouses across the nation until being eclipsed by the Fresnel lens during the 1850s. To perform the actual construction of the Fort Gratiot Light's tower and keeper's quarters, Lewis subcontracted the work to Daniel Warren, of Rochester, New York. Additional funding was acquired during

The steamer *Delaware* is about to enter the St. Clair River as it transits the lower reaches of Lake Huron. In the background, the Fort Gratiot Lighthouse performs its role in providing a navigational beacon, thus enabling ships to pass safely through this area, ca. 1910. (Library of Congress)

Another view of the Fort Gratiot Lighthouse, this time from the shore, looking north, ca. 1910. (Library of Congress)

the spring of 1825 when Congress appropriated a further $5,000 for the project in April of that year.

Construction of the Fort Gratiot light was completed on August 8, 1825. Located at approximately the same location at which the first Blue Water Bridge now stands, the tower stood 32 feet in height, and measured 18 feet in diameter at its base and 9 ½ feet at its top. The light was originally operated by Rufus Hatch and Jean B. Desnoyers, whom were replaced by George McDougall of Detroit upon his arrival on December 2, 1825. McDougall had been appointed as the Fort Gratiot Lighthouse's keeper only after pulling some political strings. All written accounts of George McDougall describe him as being a large man. As such, he found the lighthouse's steep stairs and small trap door, measuring 18 inches by 21 ¼ inches, much to his disliking. To perform the majority of the duties required to maintain the lighthouse, McDougall hired an assistant that he paid out of his own pocket, as the government refused to allocate funds for an assistant keeper.

The Fort Gratiot Light was poorly constructed, and by the summer of 1828, cracks began appearing in its walls leading to the tower tilting towards the east. These structural deficiencies were magnified further by erosion of the ground the lighthouse was built upon. In such a condition, it was only a matter of time before the structure would be pushed past its breaking point. Such an event occurred in September of 1828, when the lighthouse was severely damaged by a storm, leading to its complete collapse in November of that year.

Following the destruction of the lighthouse, Congress acted swiftly by approving the expenditure of $8,000 on March 2, 1829 for the building of a replacement. This new structure was to be built at a more suitable location, on the shore of Lake Huron just north of the entrance to the St. Clair River. In April 1829, Lucius Lyon was contracted to build the new Fort Gratiot Lighthouse.[2]

Composed of brick, the new tower was completed in December 1829 and reached 74 feet in height with a base diameter of 25 feet. George McDougall remained the official keeper of the Fort Gratiot Lighthouse until his death in October 1842. In 1861, the tower was heightened to its present height of 86 feet, and in 1874 new quarters, also made of brick, were constructed for the lighthouse's keeper and his assistant. This latter position having been approved by the government in June of 1870.

Fueled by the economic growth of the nation, commerce on the Great Lakes expanded dramatically during the last half of the nineteenth century. This made the confluence of the St. Clair River and Lake Huron one of the busiest waterways in the world, and gave new importance to the Fort Gratiot Lighthouse's role of guiding ships on their passages through this area.

Storms on the Great Lakes are notorious for their severity, and during its long career, the Fort Gratiot Lighthouse had endured many such storms. During the Great Storm of 1913, perhaps the most ferocious of all of the storms to strike the lakes in recorded history, the lighthouse withstood a serious pounding from heavy wave action.

Over the years, several improvements have been made to the Fort Gratiot Lighthouse, including the installation of a steam powered fog signal in 1901 that was housed inside of its own brick structure. In 1931, the government purchased three acres of land adjacent to the lighthouse where a new United States Coast Guard station was opened the following year.

A significant improvement to the Fort Gratiot Lighthouse occurred in 1933 when it was fitted with a fully automated DCB-Aerobeacon. Manufactured by the Carlisle and Finch Company, this installation replaced a lens installed in 1867 that had been removed from the Point aux Barques Light. In 1971, the

The Fort Gratiot Lighthouse emits a flashing beacon every six seconds to mariners on lower Lake Huron, a service it has provided since its construction in 1829. The condition of the lighthouse in this 2012 photograph illustrates the culmination of restoration efforts to reopen the historical structure to the public. (Author's Photo)

Michigan Historical Commission listed the Fort Gratiot Lighthouse as an historic site.

In 2004, the Coast Guard's Port Huron station moved into new headquarters located alongside the Fort Gratiot Lighthouse. During 2005, the National Park Service recommended the transfer of the lighthouse to the city of Port Huron under the auspices of the National Historic Lighthouse Preservation Act.[3] Due to its deteriorating condition and the danger of falling debris, the Coast Guard was forced to close the lighthouse to visitors in August 2008. Following this, a concerted effort to restore the lighthouse began. This proved to be successful, with the Fort Gratiot Lighthouse being reopened to the public on May 19, 2012.

Now the oldest surviving lighthouse in Michigan, the Fort Gratiot Light continues to serve as an aid to navigation with its green beacon flashing every six seconds and reaching up to twenty-one miles into Lake Huron.[4]

# Chapter Eleven
## New Gnadenhutten

The Revolutionary War had a profound impact upon the Native Americans belonging to the Delaware Nation that inhabited the river valleys of Ohio. Pursuing a position of neutrality in the conflict placed the Delaware between two rival factions, as the hostile settlers of Pennsylvania and Virginia bordered its lands to the east, while this same region also served as a primary travel path for those tribes loyal to the British.

Living amongst the Delaware at this time was a Moravian missionary by the name of Reverend David Zeisberger. Born at Zauchtenthal, Moravia on April 11, 1721, Zeisberger had first come to the New World when he arrived in Georgia during 1738.[1] The following year, he was involved in the establishment of a Moravian mission at Bethlehem, Pennsylvania. He later became fluent in the Onondaga language, a tribe by which he was adopted and known by a name signifying "On the Pumpkin."[2]

During the last half of the eighteenth century, Moravian missionaries made their way into the wilderness to the west of Bethlehem to form new missions, primarily among the Delaware Indians. Incorporating himself with the Delaware, Zeisberger garnered much respect among most of the tribes that he encountered. He later used his influence during a council of Delaware braves when he successfully argued against an alliance with the British during the Revolutionary War.

In the fall of 1781, this position of neutrality influenced an order issued by the British headquarters in the northwest at Fort

The Reverend David Zeisberger preaches to a group of Indians gathered around a campfire in this engraving made from an 1862 painting by Christian Schussele. (Library of Congress)

Detroit to remove the Delaware Indians from their lands in Ohio. Forced to leave their villages, and forbidden to return, the Indians were left in a state of destitution.

In October of that same year, Major Arent Schuyler De Peyster, the British commandant at the fort, ordered the Moravian missionaries in Ohio to Detroit.[3] There they were to answer charges of sympathizing with the American cause. Answering this summons was David Zeisberger, with fellow missionaries John Heckewelder, Gottlieb Sensemann, and William Edwards. This party, which also included five Delaware Indians, endured a difficult journey to Detroit, as it was ill equipped for such an endeavor.

Upon their arrival, Major De Peyster initially behaved contemptuously towards the Moravian missionaries. This was to change, however, after the missionaries had been largely vindicated of the complicity charges, after which the British commander treated them with kindness. The Moravians were detained at Detroit for several weeks, during which De Peyster and the Indian agents attempted to persuade them to support the British cause.[4] Refusing to take up arms for either side, the Moravians were sent back to Ohio. There they, and their converts, would spend the winter camped out near Upper Sandusky under the guardianship of Half-King, head chief of the Wyandot.

In March 1782, after enduring several months of cold weather and hunger, ninety-six of the displaced Christianized Indians were allowed to return to their former lands to gather standing corn. Consisting mostly of Delaware Indians, this group was subsequently taken prisoner by a group of American militiamen, which blamed them for atrocities against the settlers that had been committed primarily by the Wyandot. In the resulting violence, that occurred on March 8, 1782, only two of the original ninety-six Indians prisoners managed to escape being killed.[5]

In March 1782, Major De Peyster issued orders calling for the Moravian missionaries, and their families, to be brought to Detroit. Fearing for their safety, the British commander was determined to either keep the Moravians at Detroit, or send them back to Bethlehem, Pennsylvania. In the end, however, De Peyster allowed the Moravians to establish a new mission on a tract of land secured from the Chippewa Indians northeast of Detroit. There they and their Christianized Indians would be out of the path of warring tribes.

On July 20, 1782, a group of twenty-five persons, including David Zeisberger, John Jungmann, and their wives, set sail from Detroit heading north towards the River Huron, which is known today as the Clinton River. It would not be until the following evening that they reached their destination a few miles up the river, which empties into Lake St. Clair.[6]

As required by the church, Zeisberger maintained a diary in which he noted his initial disappointment with the land bordering the meandering river, which he found to be swampy and infested with mosquitoes. After conducting numerous landings along the river to inspect the surrounding countryside, the settlers finally found a suitable location on the evening of July 22, 1782. [7]

The site chosen for the new settlement lay on the south side of the river, across from present day Mt. Clemens, and appeared to have been previously occupied by an Indian village. Evidence of this can be found in an entry that Zeisberger made in his diary on July 23, 1782:

A small monument honoring the Moravian Mission dedicated during 1913 by the Daughters of the American Revolution and now placed in the Clinton Grove Cemetery, just outside of Mt. Clemens. (Author's Photo)

"We found many traces that a long time ago an Indian town must have stood on this place, for we saw many holes in the ground, which were now indeed filled up, but quite recognizable, in which Indians have even now the custom of keeping their corn and other property."

Tents, originally pitched by the Moravians when they first arrived, quickly gave way to rudimentary huts within a few days. In time, cabins were built in two rows, one on each side of a single street, with each of the buildings having approximately fifty feet of frontage. While devotion to a doctrine of peace prevented the Moravians from building any blockhouse or stockade at their new settlement, it did not prevent them from adding meager fortifications to their small chapel.[8]

It appears that the Moravian settlement remained nameless during its early days, as it is not referred to as Gnadenhutten in Zeisberger's diary until September 4, 1783. Meaning, "The Tents of Grace," this name was a favorite of the Moravian missionaries as it was used in no fewer than five of their missions established in America.[9] Subsequent historical accounts of Moravian missions began referring to the Michigan settlement as New Gnadenhutten, a name by which it is now commonly known.

Early in the settlement's history, the Moravians enjoyed good relations with their British and Chippewa neighbors. Zeisberger provides many compliments in his diary concerning the generosity afforded the Moravians by Major De Peyster, whom he credits with supplying enough food for the missionaries and their Christianized Indians until they could harvest enough food to provide for themselves. Cordial relations with the British would be maintained following De Peyster's departure from Fort Detroit in May 1784.

By the spring of 1783, however, relations with the Chippewa Indians had become strained. The Chippewa's eagerness for the Moravians to depart was related in a letter sent to Fort Detroit in

May of that year. In his diary, Zeisberger writes that Major De Peyster responded that the Moravians should continue with their planting, as he would arrange a satisfactory solution with the Chippewa Indians.[10]

Hunting and fishing in the country surrounding New Gnadenhutten was excellent, and by the summer of 1783, the first crops planted in the fields became available. The settlement's Indian residents also produced canoes, baskets, brooms, bowls, ladles, and other marketable items, which were in demand at nearby Fort Detroit.[11]

The harsh winter of 1783-84 placed new hardships on the residents of New Gnadenhutten, the severity of which can be ascertained from the following excerpts from Zeisberger's diary beginning on January 24, 1784:

In 1972, the Michigan Historical Commission registered the Moravian Road as its historical site #142. In recognition of this status, a state historical marker was erected at the intersection of Moravian Road and 16 Mile Road in Clinton Township.
(Author's Photo)

> "This week it snowed several days in succession, and the snow was now three feet deep, so that it was hard to get firewood."

A few days later, as winter continued its deadly onslaught, Zeisberger made the following entry into his journal:

> "It has snowed nearly every day, and the snow gets ever deeper. Our Indian brethren, about whom we are most anxious and distressed, have many of them, nothing to eat... No one had thought there would be such a winter. Old settlers in Detroit say that as long as they have lived there the snow has never been so deep."[12]

Following the cruel winter, the spring and summer of 1784 witnessed southeast Michigan enduring a severe famine, with many residents of Fort Detroit surviving by cooking weeds. The shortage of food was further amplified by the loss of many cattle to wolves. The famine would not be fully alleviated until the harvest in September of that year.[13]

During early 1785, the Chippewa Indians, still resenting the Moravian settlement on their lands, made new demands for the settlers to leave. While some consideration was given to abandoning New Gnadenhutten during the spring of 1785, the Moravians, fearing that they were destined to live as refugees if they could not remain at their permanent settlement, decided to remain.

On December 19, 1785, some of the Christianized Indians began to lay out a new path through the wilderness leading from New Gnadenhutten to Detroit, which was capable of handling wagon traffic. Measuring twenty-three and one-half miles in length when completed, and named the "Moravian Road," this passage was the first interior road built in Michigan.[14]

While the Chippewa Indians had permitted the Moravians to settle on their lands to escape persecution during the Revolutionary War, the restoration of peace renewed demands for them to leave. By early 1786, this resentment had reached a boiling point, prompting the British commander at Detroit, Major William Ancrum, to acquiesce to appeals from the Chippewa by informing the Moravians not to clear any additional land.[15]

Complying with the wishes of the Chippewa, the Moravian settlers departed New Gnadenhutten on April 20, 1786. Prior to leaving, John Heckewelder had asked many leading citizens of Detroit, among whom was merchant John Askin, to petition Major Ancrum in an effort to compensate the settlers for their homes. To this end, Ancrum, in a joint letter with John Askin declared that they would advance £200 on the prospective sale of the houses. The same correspondence also promised the Moravians protection and safe conduct to their destination upon their departure.

The Moravians left New Gnadenhutten in twenty-two canoes bound for Detroit. From there, they departed on April 28, 1786 aboard the sloops *Beaver* and *Mackinaw* destined for the Cuyahoga River, where the city of Cleveland would later be built. After spending four long weeks on Lake Erie, the Moravians finally arrived at the mouth of the Cuyahoga, where they remained for a short time.[16] After further travels, some members remained in Ohio, while others eventually settled in Canada.

David Zeisberger lived for a time in Canada at the Fairfield Mission in what would become southern Ontario. In October 1798, Zeisberger, his wife and 33 converts traveled to central Ohio to found a new mission along the Muskingum River at Goshen, Ohio. This mission was built on land granted to the Moravians by the US Congress in 1788. Zeisberger would live out his final days at Goshen before dying there on November 17, 1808 at the age of 87 years.

Meanwhile, following the abandonment of New Gnadenhutten, the only white settlers remaining in the area belonged to the family of Richard Conner, whom had settled there in March 1783. The Conner family possessed an intimate understanding of Indian customs, therefore the Chippewa made no effort to force their removal. Richard Conner would spend the remainder of his life at the Moravian settlement until his death on April 17, 1808.

In time, the New Gnadenhutten site became known as Casino, and later as Frederick. By 1818, this community had grown to include twenty families. The building of sawmills in the area led to Frederick becoming the busiest port on the Clinton River by 1843. Such prosperity continued until 1852 when the sawmills were destroyed by fire, leading to the dissolution of Frederick shortly thereafter.

# Chapter Twelve
## The Burning of Holland - 1871

During 1871, the month of October witnessed widespread destruction descending upon the Midwest with several major fires erupting nearly simultaneously in Illinois, Wisconsin, and Michigan. Undoubtedly, the most well known of these was the Great Chicago Fire, which began on Sunday, October 8, 1871. This blaze, however, was just one of many that threatened to destroy numerous cities in the Great Lakes region during that week. Some 200 miles to the north of Chicago, on the shores of Green Bay, the area surrounding Peshtigo, Wisconsin burned so completely that over 1,500 people lost their lives. This death toll was at least five times greater than that experienced at Chicago, and remains to this day the worst fire in United States history.[1]

Across the lake, fire also swept through Manistee, Michigan on October 8, destroying over half of that city and leaving approximately 1,000 homeless. That same day, on the opposite side of the state, Port Huron suffered considerable damage when a blaze swept through the city, killing at least fifty people.

During the afternoon of Sunday, October 8, 1871, a fine ash began falling from the sky over Holland, Michigan.[2] Unbeknownst to the city's 2,400 residents, this ash represented both their first indicator of the Chicago Fire and as an omen of the devastation that soon would lay waste to the city that they had labored to build since its founding nearly twenty-five years earlier.

In the weeks leading up to early October, the Midwest had experienced a continuation of an extreme drought that had begun during the summer. The lack of rain, combined with unseasonably warm temperatures created conditions that made much of Michigan a tinderbox. In fact, in the week preceding the burning of Holland, the city had narrowly escaped destruction after several fires broke out in the surrounding woods.[3]

Around 2 o'clock in the afternoon of October 8, the fire alarm first sounded in the southwest section of the city. This area had recently been opened up for settlement, and was therefore sparsely populated and heavily wooded. Blowing from the southwest, and gradually increasing in intensity, the wind aided the spread of the fire. Initial fire fighting efforts concentrated on the wooded tracts in the south and southwest of Holland in an attempt to halt the advancing flames.

As night approached, the wind continued to increase in velocity as it pushed the fire closer to the heart of the city. Among the first structures to fall victim to the fire was the Cappen & Bertch Tannery in the western section of the city, which with its huge bark piles was an easy prey for the advancing blaze. In the southern part of the city, the Third Reformed Church was another early casualty to the growing fire.[4]

The burning of these two structures contributed to the spread of the fire. As the tannery burned, the wind, which by this time had shifted to the west, carried several pieces of burning bark towards the center of Holland, where it ignited new fires. As the Third Reformed Church succumbed to the flames, many of its shingles and much of its siding were blown towards the city's interior, creating a trail of fire in its wake.

So rapid was the advance of the inferno that nearly the entire city of Holland was destroyed between one and three o'clock in the morning of October 9, 1871. For those living in the area, there were few avenues of escape. One of these was the grounds of Hope College, which had remained untouched by the flames.

Meanwhile, many others escaped annihilation by taking small boats into nearby Black Lake.

The desperation of those attempting to flee the sweeping flames is revealed in the following excerpt taken from *The Janesville Gazette* printed on October 14, 1871:

> One woman, on leaving her house, had tied her baby in a bundle, but in her hurry[,] she took the wrong bundle, and to her dismay discovered her mistake when it appeared to be too late. Of seven children[,] she could only find two. Fortunately, however, the bundle containing the live baby was picked up in the street all right, and it was believed that the other children were also found.

As devastating as the Holland fire was, it was fortunate that only one life is known to have been lost in the disaster. This is in stark contrast to the other such incidents that occurred in the Great Lakes region during the same time. Due to the lack of accurate information emanating from the burnt out city, early newspaper stories concerning the fire reported a much higher death toll than had actually occurred. As late as October 12, three days after the event, a story appearing in the *Racine County Argus* related that at least five individuals had perished in the flames.

The morning of October 9, 1871, revealed that the fire had dealt a devastating blow to Holland. The list of destruction included 210 homes, 75 shops and offices, 15 factories, 5 churches, 3 hotels, and 45 miscellaneous structures in the city. On the waterfront, five docks and warehouses had also been consumed by the fire, along with one tug and a number of boats. The total amount of property destroyed was valued at $900,000, of which only $35,000 was covered by insurance, which for the most part was never received as the Great Chicago Fire had rendered most of the insurance companies bankrupt.[5] The rapid spread of the fire also caused the death of over 250 farm animals including horses, cows, and hogs.

All told, over three hundred families were left homeless by the fire. With only thirty houses still standing in the city, the survivors were in desperate need of assistance. The transportation of relief supplies into the area, however, was further complicated by the fact that the rail line entering Holland had been cut off by the fires of earlier that week. Assistance in conveying these badly needed supplies to the devastated city was provided by residents from the surrounding area, including those from Grand Haven.

While many of the provisions reaching Holland were supplied by bakeries and grocery stores, the nature of some relief supplies represented the kindness generated by anonymous strangers. Examples of this included, among other things, a partly cut loaf of bread, a single biscuit, a part of a ham, and a remnant of a roast.[6] While appearing somewhat archaic by today's standards, such donations at the time likely represented a portion of a family's meal that was given up to feed an unknown person in desperate need.

On the afternoon of Wednesday October 11, 1871, a meeting was called to discuss the situation in Holland. Among those in attendance was the Reverend Albertus Van Raalte, whom had originally founded the community when he arrived in Ottawa County with a group of followers in 1847. During an inspirational speech before the citizens gathered there that day, Rev. Van Raalte, expressed, "With our Dutch tenacity and our American experience, Holland will be rebuilt."

Although hampered by the rise in the cost of building supplies brought about by the Chicago Fire, work on rebuilding the city began shortly afterwards. The elevated cost of materials, however, caused the reconstruction efforts to cost significantly more than had been originally envisioned. To add insult to injury, a financial panic during 1873 effectively reduced the valuation of property in the city by fifty percent.

In time, however, Holland rose above the ashes left by the 1871 fire to become one of the more vibrant cities in Michigan. Renowned for its rich Dutch heritage, Holland has grown to become one of the most visited communities in the state, and the home to over 34,000 residents.

# Chapter Thirteen
## Michigan's Most Unique Island

The island of Isle Royale is the northernmost territory belonging to the state of Michigan. Measuring 45 miles in length and with a width of 9 miles at its widest point, the island contains an area equal to 207 square miles. Located in Lake Superior, 52 miles northwest of Copper Harbor, this island actually lies much closer to Minnesota and Ontario, Canada, than it does to the state in which it is incorporated. In fact, Isle Royale sits only six miles inside of the international border between the United States and its northern neighbor.

Isle Royale National Park consists of more than 450 islets, surrounded by numerous rock outcroppings. The combined land area of the park is approximately 843 square miles, with Mount Desor, rising 791 feet above the level of the lake, being its highest point. With the heat of summer tempered by the cool waters of Lake Superior, spruce and balsam fir are forest species commonly found along the shoreline areas. Meanwhile, red and sugar maples, yellow birch, and northern red oak dominate the elevated regions of the island's interior.[1]

In terms of geology, Isle Royale, sitting on the western edge of the Lake Superior Syncline shares much in common with the Keweenaw Peninsula that represents the eastern extension of that geological formation. As result, rock, including native copper, found in both of these landmasses is of the same age and characteristics.

Following the end of the American Revolution, Britain ceded Isle Royale to the United States in 1783. The British, however, maintained control over the island until the end of the War of

1812. An abundance of fish, including herring, trout, and whitefish in the waters around the island led to the beginning of commercial fishing operations during the early years of the nineteenth century. During the later years of the 1830s, the American Fur Company erected seven fishing stations on Isle Royale. However, the Panic of 1837, a period of economic recession that lasted until 1843, severely affected these operations by diminishing their markets.

The first Europeans to arrive on Isle Royale were by no means the first pioneers to step foot on the island. Around 2,000 B.C., Indians began mining native copper on Isle Royale, a fact bore out by the abundance of ancient mine pits around the island. Although a precise number of these pits has never been determined, some estimates have calculated that there are as many as 5,000 such excavations scattered around the island. The Indians used the copper for ornamental purposes along with the manufacture of spears, knives, and various other implements. Native American activity on Isle Royale peaked between 800 and 1600, when the arrival of Europeans into the Great Lakes region began to disrupt their culture.

During the mid-1840s, Michigan experienced a mining boom following the discovery of large copper reserves in the Upper Peninsula. With similar geologic features, it was natural for copper prospecting to spread to Isle Royale, leading to the beginning of the first modern mining operations on the island. By this time, the only remaining Indian settlements consisted of a seasonal fishing camp on Grace Island, and a maple sugar encampment at Sugar Mountain.

The remote nature of Isle Royale along with the inhospitable weather conditions prevalent throughout the winter months on Lake Superior combined to restrict the profitability of mining on the island. Located in small veins, the copper deposits themselves complicated their economical extraction. These factors prevented any of the mining ventures operating on Isle Royale during the last half of the nineteenth century from taking considerable quantities of copper from the island. Of the mining concerns operating on Isle Royale during the 1840-1850 timeframe, the most successful was the Siskowit Mining Company. Between 1849 and 1855, this firm successfully extracted 95 tons of copper from the isolated island.[2]

Between 1873 and 1881, a renewed interest in mining copper on Isle Royale took place. The largest concern to operate on the island during this period was the Minong Mining Company, which operated the Minong Mine near McCargoe Cove. During the peak of its operation, this firm employed approximately 150 men. Along with their families, these miners established a settlement on the island that included a blacksmith shop, stamp mill, and a dock.

One final attempt at exploiting Isle Royale's mineral resources took place between 1889 and 1893 in the Windigo area. This led to the establishment of a small settlement at Washington Harbor. An extensive program of drilling, however, once again revealed that the copper deposits were insufficient to prove economically viable for reclamation. This marked the end of mining operations on Isle Royale, an activity stretching back 4,000 years.

Given its remoteness and lack of extensive forests, Isle Royale is ill suited to support a large-scale commercial logging industry. This, however, did not prevent some cutting of white cedar and pine along Washington Creek during the 1890s by a firm based out of Duluth, Minnesota. After cutting, the logs were floated downstream to Washington Harbor, where booms held them rafted together in preparation for towing across the lake. This operation came to a swift conclusion when a storm flooded out Washington Creek, thus allowing the logs to break free and float into Lake Superior.

As commerce on Lake Superior grew during the late 1800s, Isle Royale, with its numerous islands and reefs, posed a serious danger to mariners sailing the northernmost of the Great Lakes. This was particularly true for vessels bound for, or departing, Port Arthur and Fort William, Ontario. Later combined to form present day Thunder Bay, these two cities were among the busiest Canadian ports on the Great Lakes.

Since the nineteenth century, dozens of shipwrecks have occurred on and around Isle Royale. Between the late 1800s and 1947, ships of all types met their fates in the hazardous waters surrounding the island. This list of casualties includes everything from large steel steamers to small fishing vessels. As such, Isle Royale has become a popular location for scuba divers, with over 1,000 dives taking place in the National Park on an annual basis.

An early example of a steel-hulled steamer meeting with disaster on the shores of Isle Royale is the loss of the *Algoma* in

The steamer *Algoma* arrives in port with a coating of ice after weathering a storm on Lake Superior. (Author's Collection)

After stranding on the rocks off Isle Royale on November 7, 1885, the *Algoma* broke apart, leaving only the stern visible above the waters of Lake Superior. (Author's Collection)

November 1885. Built in Scotland and owned by the Canadian Pacific Railroad, this combination freight and passenger vessel had entered service the previous year. Departing Owen Sound, Ontario on November 5, 1885, under the command of Captain John Moore, the *Algoma* first transited Georgian Bay, then Lake Huron and the St. Marys River before finally entering Lake Superior. Heralding the beginning of the winter season on the lakes, the month of November is infamous for its storms. This occasion was to be no different as the *Algoma*, along with its passengers and crew, ran into a fierce gale on the evening of November 6, 1885.

During the next several hours, the 262 foot steamer continued to slowly push her way through the storm. By the early hours of November 7, Captain Moore, unsure of his current position and realizing the danger posed by Isle Royale as his ship neared the western end of Lake Superior, decided to turn towards the open lake shortly after 4 o'clock in the morning. It was during this maneuver, however, that the *Algoma* struck Greenstone Rock off the northeastern end of Isle Royale.

With its stern impaled upon the rocks and its bow floating free, a tremendous amount of strain was placed upon the hull. Not designed to withstand such forces, the *Algoma* snapped in two just forward of the engine room, the forward section sinking in deep water. Meanwhile, the stern remained stranded on the reef, thereby providing a refuge for Captain Moore and thirteen other survivors.

Assisted from the wreck by local fishermen living on Isle Royale, the 14 survivors were finally rescued on November 9, two days after the wreck, by one of the *Algoma*'s fleet mates, the steamer *Athabasca*. All told, at least 38 were killed in the accident, making this Lake Superior's most costly shipwreck in terms of the number of lives lost.[3]

Not all of the wrecks located in the waters around Isle Royale took place during storms, nor do all involve significant losses of life. On June 7, 1928, while outbound from Washington Harbor, the 190-foot passenger steamer *America* stuck a reef just after leaving the dock. Immediately following the accident, which occurred at 3 AM, the *America* began slowly sinking by the stern.

The slowness of the sinking allowed an orderly evacuation by the 30 man crew and 15 passengers in the *America*'s lifeboats, all of which safely reached shore. By 4:30 AM, ninety minutes after stranding, the steamer was mostly underwater, with only its bow section extending sharply above the surface. Over time, the wreck of the *America* slipped deeper into the water, finally reaching its present location with its bow clearly visible just a few feet below the clear waters of the lake.

As navigational equipment improved during the early twentieth century, the danger of Isle Royale, and its countless reefs, receded as the number of shipwrecks declined. The last major shipwreck to occur on the reefs surrounding Isle Royale took place on June 4, 1947, when the Canada Steamship Lines' *Emperor* struck the Canoe Rocks. Shortly after stranding, the stern of the 525 foot vessel quickly foundered after its hull broke at the number 4 hatch. Twelve crewmembers, including the captain, lost their lives in the accident, the blame of which was subsequently laid upon the first mate.[4]

As the passages around Isle Royale remain a main thoroughfare for ships bound or departing from the busy ports of western Lake Superior, the area remains a navigational hazard that demands the utmost respect even in modern times. On November 24, 1990, the crew of the *Kinsman Independent* was reminded of this fact when their ship ran aground just over a quarter-mile southwest of Isle Royale Light at the head of Siskiwit Bay, on the eastern shores of Isle Royale.[5] Operated by the Kinsman Lines of Buffalo, New York, the 642 foot steamer suffered an estimated $2 million in damages during the incident, which resulted from a navigational error.

When the steamer *Emperor* ran onto the Canoe Rocks in June 1947, it became the last major shipwreck to occur in the waters immediately surrounding Isle Royale. (Author's Collection)

People have been visiting Isle Royale to enjoy the solitude of the remote location since the 1860s. As the population of the Midwest grew at an exceptional rate during the early 1900s, Isle Royale experienced a corresponding rise in popularity as a tourist destination. Easily accessible by lake steamer, the abundant fishing and tranquil wilderness offered by the island were much in demand for those endeavoring to escape, at least temporarily, the noise and excitement of the bustling cities.

The influx of tourists to the island led to the building of resorts at Belle Isle, Rock Harbor, Tobin Harbor, Windigo, and Washington Island. In addition to those attracted to the island by the resorts, many other visitors built vacation cottages, many of which were located on the northeast end of Isle Royale.

The exploitive nature of human activity on Isle Royale during the late 1800s caused serious ecological damage. Much of the damage caused during this period can be attributed to the activities of the copper miners, which used fire to reduce the island's forest cover. Although the cessation of such activities allowed the island's forests to begin recovering, a growing movement to preserve the uniqueness of Isle Royale began during the early twentieth century .

This was in response to the plans by some landowners to begin new lumbering and mining activities on the island. A major figure in the movement opposing this was Albert Stoll, Jr., the conservation editor of the *Detroit News*. In 1921, Albert Stoll, supported by the paper's editor in chief, George E. Miller, proposed that the newspaper launch a campaign to save the island from exploitive activities.[6] While early ambitions advocated the island becoming a state preserve, subsequent efforts focused upon having Isle Royale, and its surrounding waters, designated as a national park. In 1922, Michigan Representative Louis C. Cramton made just such a proposal to the United States Congress. This began a long period of debate

The idyllic charm of Isle Royale is apparent in this photograph of the Rock Harbor Guest House, completed in 1924. (Library of Congress)

between those in favor of such a status for Isle Royale, and those in opposition to such a move.

As Congress continued to debate the island's national park status, archeological activities on Isle Royale continued to produce new insights into the island's history. In 1924, the Milwaukee Public Museum sponsored an archeological expedition to the island, this being followed in 1928 by the McDonald-Massee Expedition. The latter undertaking was led by noted polar explorer Eugene F. McDonald, whom was one of three original founders of the Zenith Radio Corporation.

Consisting of three yachts, the McDonald-Massee Expedition departed Chicago on July 21, 1928 bound for Isle Royale. The expedition quickly ran into trouble, however, when one of its yachts, the *Swastika*, was damaged by a waterspout in Lake Michigan the following day. With her mainmast split, the *Swastika* limped into Manitowoc, Wisconsin for repairs before continuing her voyage up the lakes two days later. The following excerpt describing the trouble experienced by the expedition was printed in the July 28, 1928 edition of *The Manitowoc Herald-News*:

> The Isle Royal[e] Archeological expedition consisting of the Naroca, the Margo[,] and the Swastika under the command of Eugene F. MacDonald[*sic*], noted polar explorer, and with a number of scientists in the party plans to explore the 250,000 acres of wilderness on the northern Lake Superior isle. But[,] after some of the crew saw three waterspouts and a triple rainbow in the storm of Sunday afternoon some of the sailors felt like deserting the expedition.

These early difficulties behind it, the expedition succeeded in reaching the remote island, where it made a general survey of the remains in various areas of Isle Royale, while also conducting a series of exploratory excavations. One of the findings made during the expedition was the discovery of an ossuary near Point Houghton, from which the remains of at least twelve persons were removed.[7] The archeological value of Isle Royale compelled the McDonald-Massee Expedition to send a radiogram from the *Naroca* to President Calvin Coolidge stressing the importance of the island becoming a national park or monument. The expedition also went so far as to invite the President to visit the island for a personal tour.[8] As there is no record of President Coolidge ever making such a journey, it appears, in the end, that this invitation was not acted upon.[9]

After years of wrangling, the US Congress finally passed a bill in 1931 designating Isle Royale as a national park project. This allowed for the purchase of land and the construction of the infrastructure necessary for the island to operate as a park. On April 3, 1940, the Isle Royale National Park was formally established. Delayed by the Second World War, however, the

A moose swims in the waters surrounding Isle Royale. The interaction between this animal and the island's wolf population has been the subject of a scientific study that began in 1958. (National Park Service)

park's official dedication did not take place until six years later on August 27, 1946.

As a national park, human activity on Isle Royale was restricted, with only a few families being allowed to maintain cottages on the island. Meanwhile, the park's wildlife has undergone a number of changes since the beginning of the 1900s. This includes the disappearance of the woodland caribou during the 1920s, which corresponded with a rise in the number of moose on the island during the same timeframe. During the 1930s, the moose population was thinned considerably by starvation and a program by the Michigan Conservation Department in which 72 animals were captured for relocation. By 1937, it was estimated that there were only 200 to 300 moose remaining on Isle Royale, a number that was estimated at the time would produce a future herd of 1,000 or more.[10]

During the winter of 1949, wolves first arrived on Isle Royale by crossing an ice bridge extending from the Canadian shore. By coincidence, this event came at a time in which park officials were considering the introduction of wolves to the island in an effort to control the moose population. Prior to the arrival of wolves, the moose had no natural predator on the isolated island, which allowed their numbers to soar, thus opening up the possibility of widespread starvation among the species.

Durward Allen, a wildlife ecologist from Purdue University, realizing that the single predator-prey interaction between the wolf and moose in a closed ecosystem presented a unique opportunity, originated a program to study this relationship in 1958. Continuing to this day, this project has become the longest such program taking place in the world. Numbering no more than 50 animals at any given time since their arrival, Isle Royale has never supported a large population of wolves. In recent years, however, even these modest numbers have witnessed a sharp decline, so that by early 2012 there were only nine wolves known to be living on the island. This reduction in wolf population included a discovery made early that year of three animals having been killed after falling into an abandoned mine shaft. With a shortage of females, officials were debating during the summer of 2012 whether to reintroduce more wolves onto the island, or to allow nature to take its course.[11]

While some commercial fishing still takes place in the waters around Isle Royale, there are no permanent residents living on the island. Furthermore, tourism to the park is open to the public only during a period extending from mid-April to the end of October. Protected from further human encroachment and possessing some of the most unspoiled wilderness in the state, the Isle Royale National Park represents an integral, and unique, component of Michigan's past and future.

# Chapter Fourteen
## The Alpena Excursion Train Wreck - 1902

On the morning of June 8, 1902, passengers began boarding a train at Alpena, which would carry them on an excursion 115 miles to the south at Saginaw. Sponsored by the German Aid Society of Alpena, this outing had attracted more than 500 attendees. Operated by the Detroit & Mackinac Railway, the train ferrying the excursionists consisted of a steam engine and twelve coaches.[1]

At 7:15 AM, that Sunday morning, the locomotive's engineer, identified only by the name of Hopper, put the train in motion as it departed Alpena to begin its journey south. With smoke bellowing from its stack, the steam engine struggled to pick up speed as it left the city to follow the Detroit & Mackinac Railway's rail line extending along the shores of Lake Huron. During its journey to Saginaw, the excursion train would pass through Black River, which is located about 20 miles south of Alpena. While the excursion thus far had been without incident, this was about to change as the train reached this small community.

Without warning, and while traveling at 40 miles per hour near Black River, the steam engine's tender suddenly jumped the tracks. An instant later, Engineer Hopper placed the engine into reverse while also engaging his airbrakes in a desperate attempt to slow the train to a stop. Unfortunately, the momentum of a train traveling at high speed is not easily controlled. Therefore, the forces generated by Hopper's efforts to halt the speeding train tore up 200 feet of track and caused the first three coaches to detach and derail.

After leaving the tracks, the three cars careened into a nearby ditch. Containing approximately 40 passengers, the first coach was cut in half by the two cars following it. When the railcars finally came to a stop, all three were intermingled in a pile of wreckage. Despite the level of carnage, only one passenger was killed in the crash. This was August Grosinski, whom was fatally injured when he was crushed in the wreckage of the three coaches. Seated with his father, Grosinski's young son was extremely lucky to escape the wreck unharmed.[2]

In addition to the single fatality, at least fifty other passengers received injuries ranging primarily from cuts and bruises to broken bones. While the vast majority of those involved in the wreck only suffered injuries of a minor nature, at least seven of their fellow travelers had been injured more severely. The following excerpt from an Associated Press report released the day after the accident appeared in the June 14, 1902 edition of *The Alton Democrat*:

> Following are the most seriously injured: John McCarthy, Alpena, left arm broken and serious internal injuries, will probably die; Ernest Legatski, Alpena, right leg broken and probably fatal internal injuries; Jacob Mondorff, Alpena, probable fatal internal injuries; Louis Peppler, Alpena, right thigh fractured; Carey Beyer, right leg broken, three toes cut off and head seriously injured.

Immediately following the accident, the Detroit & Mackinac Railway arranged to rush a number of physicians from Alpena to Black River aboard a special train. This included Drs. Edward E. McKnight, William A. Secrist, and Otto Bertram, along with five other surgeons. Accompanying the medical staff to the wreck site was C. W. Luce, a superintendent from the railroad company.[3]

Upon arriving at the accident scene, the injured were made as comfortable as possible before being placed aboard a train for the return trip to Alpena. Upon their arrival back in the city, many of the injured returned to their homes, while those with injuries of a more severe nature were taken to the Alpena Hospital. While many of these patients experienced hospital stays of less than two weeks, a few were not released until four weeks after the accident.

Contrary to the early media reports, it appears that none of the injured died immediately following the accident. Further confirmation of August Grosinski as being the only fatality attributed to the incident can be found in court documents pertaining to a lawsuit brought against the Detroit & Mackinac Railway Company by Dr. McKnight for the payment of medical services he performed as a result of the June 8, 1902 accident.[4]

# Chapter Fifteen
## The Life of a Pioneering Missionary

On June 12, 1849, the schooner *Hiram Merrill* sailed into Grand Traverse Bay destined for a remote location on the Leelanau Peninsula. Aboard this diminutive vessel that morning when it dropped anchor in the tranquil waters of the bay, was a group of fifteen settlers led by the Reverend George Nelson Smith. The spot picked for the landing was located about one mile north of the site at which this group would found a settlement, which later became known as Northport.

Born on a farm near Swanton, Vermont on October 25, 1807, George Smith became John and Esther Smith's first of many children. Marrying Esther Austin during the previous year, John Smith's family had participated in the Revolutionary War, a heritage he shared in common with that of his bride. Both of George Smith's parents were devout Calvinists.

The childhood of the one-day missionary was like that of many that grew up on the farms of that era. During the summer months, working on the family's farm consumed most of the young man's waking hours, while in the winter season he attended school. Throughout his period of growing up, George Smith knew nothing of the pleasures and possessions bestowed upon later generations.

After leaving the family farm in March 1827, at the age of nineteen years old, George Smith arrived at Highgate, Vermont, where he was to learn the trade of millwright at the firm of L. and J. Carpenter. It was during his employment here that George Smith became devoted to studying the Scriptures, an activity that would influence the future course of his life. As

Universalists, his employers, the Carpenters, made every attempt in converting the young man to their beliefs. Rather than accede to the views of his employers, however, George Smith instead delved deep into the Scriptures so that he could successfully defend against the arguments put forth by his employers. In the end, the Carpenters were unsuccessful in persuading the young George Smith to accept their beliefs.

On July 6, 1828, George Smith joined the Congregational church at Swanton. The desire to become a member of the ministry influenced his decision to leave his job on December 1, 1828 in order to devote more of his time to study. After attending school during that winter, George traveled to Canada in March 1829 to visit an uncle whom was a physician. After studying chemistry for four weeks, he returned home where, after receiving some encouragement from the Reverend E. H. Dorman, he arrived at the St. Albans Academy on May 5, 1829 to begin studying Latin.

While attending the academy during the autumn of that year, George Smith met Arvilla Almira Powers. One of Arvilla Powers' cousins was John Brown, whom later became a famous abolitionist during the 1850s. Shortly after becoming engaged to Arvilla Powers in November 1829, George Smith left Vermont to teach winter school at Russelltown in Lower Canada. Upon his return in April of the following year, George resided with Arvilla's family while she was away teaching school.

On June 15, 1830, Arvilla returned home in a state of very poor health. At the time of their engagement, it had been agreed that George would finish his studies for the ministry prior to the couple marrying. Ms. Powers' health issues, however, became a significant factor in the couple deciding to marry sooner than originally intended. Their wedding took place on July 4, 1830, when George and Arvilla were united by the Reverend Worthington Smith.

After being married, the young couple moved to Alburgh, Vermont, where they endured a period of financial hardship. While continuing with his studies for the ministry, George found work teaching in the day schools and evening singing schools. Meanwhile, his wife also contributed to the household income through teaching and sewing.[1]

During the spring of 1832, George Smith became captivated with the idea of moving westwards as the young nation expanded. Although committed to such a move, George continuing his theological studies, as such an endeavor was impractical given both his financial position, and his wife's persistent health problems. It was also during this timeframe that the couple's first child, George, was born at St. Albans on June 20, 1832.

Originally, George Smith had intended to move his small family to Ohio. These plans changed in May of 1833 when he became acquainted with a colony of Congregationalists formed for the purpose of settling in the Territory of Michigan. In the end, for reasons unknown, this colony did not proceed forward with its plans to move west. This, however, did not prevent George and Arvilla from continuing with their efforts in relocating to Michigan.

On May 8, 1833, George Smith along with his wife and young child, and Arvilla's sister, Jane Powers, departed St. Albans bound for the Territory of Michigan. During this time period, water transportation provided the most effective method of traveling into the western regions of the country. As such, this small group of settlers transited Lake Champlain by steamer before traveling by canal to Buffalo, New York. From there, they once again boarded a steamship that carried them across the length of Lake Erie to Detroit. To conserve the group's limited funds, George secured deck passage for himself aboard ship, while his wife, sister in law, and son made the voyage in a cabin.

Having but $1.06 to his credit, George Smith was faced with a severe financial hardship upon his arrival at Detroit, a situation made somewhat better following the sale of his watch for $5.50. The small group of travelers was fortunate in meeting in an old acquaintance from Vermont who helped them in obtaining a room at a nearby hotel. Later, when George Smith had found a lumber wagon willing to transport him and his family across the territory to Gull Prairie, this same friend guaranteed the $20 charged by the teamster.

After enduring a week of trekking through the wilderness by lumber wagon, the family finally arrived at Gull Prairie at the end of May. The entire trip from Vermont had consumed twenty -one days and had cost approximately $70, significantly more than originally planned.

Unable to find a house or a room to rent, and with disease running rampant in the area, the conditions greeting George Smith and his family at their destination were far from ideal. Becoming aware of their plight, a Presbyterian minister offered the family a place to stay in return for their help in erecting a barn. At the time, the minister's wife and children were ill with fever and he had been unable to find anyone to assist him in constructing the structure. After staying at the minister's residence until the fall of that year, George Smith rented a room that had formerly served as an office.

The first years in the Territory of Michigan were trying times for the group of settlers. At the time there was little in the way of construction being carried out in the southwest section of the territory. The young theology student was able find work teaching whenever possible and, at times, he found employment in the carpentry trade. Meanwhile, he also preached at every opportunity that presented itself, and during the winter of 1834, George Smith was selected to distribute bibles throughout Kalamazoo County.

During this period of Michigan history, disease was a common, but unwelcome, companion to pioneering settlers as they attempted to eke out an existence in a mostly untamed wilderness. In the spring of 1834, Arvilla became ill with fever, remaining in this state of sickness during the birth of the couple's second child, a boy that died shortly after being born. It was during this time, that her sister, Jane Powers, also came down with fever, thus causing her to return home after working as a teacher at a school a few miles away.

In August 1835, George Smith received an offer to preach in Plainwell and Otsego from the Congregational Home Missionary Society. Upon moving to Plainwell later that month, however, the family found their only shelter to be the skeletal frame of a building. Although George quickly went to work boarding up the primitive structure, there were no windows or doors available, therefore, quilts were used to cover these openings. The basic shelter also lacked a chimney, and to keep the local wolves from entering, a large fire was kept burning throughout the night.

The family lived in these quarters until its owner took possession in October. Following this, a charitable appeal garnered enough funds for an acre of land to be acquired. Assisted by a donation of lumber from a nearby mill, a house-raising took place that would see the frame of a new home being put up in one day's time. As the lumber had to be transported some fifteen miles across rudimentary roads from the mill, it took another month to get the structure boarded up. In common with their first residence in Plainwell, this building also initially lacked doors, windows, and a chimney. By the end of December, these shortcomings had been addressed by the fitting of windows and doors along with the installation of a stick chimney.

By this time, George and Arvilla's family had grown to four with the birth of a third child, a girl that they named Mary Jane. Throughout the following winter, the Smith's new home provided meager protection against the elements as its occupants struggled against starvation. Furthermore, the family's sponsor, the Congregational Home Missionary Society, was operating with only limited funding. As their home was near a heavily used crossroads, the plight of George Smith and his growing family was exacerbated by the constant arrival of tired travelers seeking both food and a temporary shelter.

On February 5, 1836, George Smith was licensed to preach at Bronson by the Presbytery of St. Joseph, Michigan. This was followed nine days later, when he conducted his first regular service at Comstock. George Smith would go on to establish further Congregational churches at Gull Prairie, Gun Plains, Otsego, and Plainwell.[2]

A little less than one year after receiving his commission to preach, on January 13, 1837, George Smith was appointed to perform missionary work. For these duties, he was granted an annual salary of $200 plus voluntary donations. Less than two weeks later, Michigan was admitted into the Union as the 26th state. That same year proved to be a busy one for George Smith as during February he participated in a state convention at Marshall of the Michigan Total Abstinence Society. His determined activities that year continued into March when he proved instrumental in the organization of the first Congregational Association in the state at Richland, a community formerly known as Gull Prairie. Among his other contributions, George Smith was responsible for in the creation of this association was the drafting of its constitution.

On April 7, 1837, George Smith was ordained by the Congregational Association by the Rev. A. S. Ware, thus making him the first such Congregational minister ordained in the state.

That same year, on October 7, the Reverend Smith made an entry into his diary that revealed his conviction for assisting the Native American population, a belief that would shape the balance of his life.

Concurrent with George Smith recording such beliefs in his diary, a delegation of Ottawa and Ojibwa Indians, under the leadership of Chiefs Shinekosche and Waukazoo, arrived from Middle Village, in Emmet County, in search of a new missionary. Dissatisfied with their Jesuit missionaries, the Indians had learned of Mr. Smith's ministerial activities during their regular migrations up and down the state.

While attending a meeting arranged to discuss the matter at Allegan, Michigan, George Smith was won over by a passionate speech made by Chief Waukazoo stating his people's desire to embrace the Protestant faith. This proved to be a turning point for the Reverend Smith as at this time he became fully committed to bringing Christianity to the Indians, remaining their true friend throughout the rest of his days.

In January 1838, another conference held at Allegan with the Native Americans, led to the establishment of the Western Society of Michigan to Benefit the Indians. In June of that same year, George Smith received an appointment as that organization's general agent. Throughout the balance of the year, the Reverend Smith pursued a program of colonization for the Indians, during which he spent much time traveling to meet various tribes in order to gain support for his plans.

By December, the colonization plans had progressed to the point that approximately thirty Indian families had joined the program. Having moved his family to a location near Allegan, the Reverend Smith delivered his first sermon on the twenty-third day of that month in a temporary structure erected especially for the service.

After becoming associated with the Indians, George Smith went about learning their language. Within a short period of time, the Reverend had become so adept with such skills that he was able to dispense with the services of an interpreter. On December 28, 1838, George Smith opened his first Indian school, which initially had only seven students in attendance. The number of students receiving instruction quickly increased, however, and soon their number had reached thirty, with ages ranging between five and fifty years old. Meanwhile, Mrs. Smith also performed teaching duties for Indian girls, during which she provided instruction on cooking and sewing in addition to reading, spelling, and writing.[3]

By the spring of 1839, the population of the colony had grown to 300 persons. On April 13 of that year, George Smith and a group of Indians departed on a survey trip to determine a suitable site for the colony's relocation. This expedition resulted in the decision to settle on the shore of the Black River at a point that is about four miles east of where the city of Holland would later be founded. During that summer, the Indians began moving to their new lands, with George Smith and his family doing likewise in August. Upon their arrival, the Smith family took up residence in a log cabin specifically built for them.

In honor of an elderly Indian, the new mission was named Old Wing. As can be expected, life at the newly established settlement was full of hardships. During the mission's first winter, food supplies came into short supply. This prompted George Smith and a neighbor, Mr. Cowles, to attempt a trip to Allegan by canoe in order to obtain supplies to last until spring. After paddling nine miles down the Black River, the two men then had to travel south on Lake Michigan in their small craft before reaching the mouth of the Kalamazoo River. After this, a trek of another twenty miles awaited George Smith and his companion before reaching Allegan. After successfully reaching their destination, and obtaining the necessary provisions, the two travelers embarked upon their return trip to the colony, where they finally arrived after a round-trip journey of three weeks in length.

The coming of spring allowed a return to improving the living conditions at the colony. Eventually, such efforts led to the construction of a large schoolhouse and the improvement of the Smith family's home. During the ten years that George Smith and his Indian wards lived at the Old Wing Mission, the Reverend fulfilled several different roles within the community. Besides the services he rendered as a preacher and educator, he was also called upon to administer medical treatments and settle disputes.

The arrival of the first Dutch settlers near Black Lake during 1847 would have a direct impact upon those living at the mission. Under the leadership of the Reverend Albertus Van Raalte, this group had arrived in New York from Holland during November of the previous year. Originally intent upon purchasing a tract of land in the Wisconsin Territory, these plans were subsequently changed to forming a settlement in western Michigan.

While conducting a prospecting tour of the region surrounding the Black River during December 1846, Van Raalte arrived at the home of George Smith. For the next three weeks, the two reverends, along with a band of Indians, surveyed the local countryside to determine its suitability for the Dutch settlers. After a brief return to Detroit, the Reverend Van Raalte arrived back at the Smith residence in February along with his family and a number of other settlers. Consisting of fifteen persons, this party was welcomed into the home of the Reverend Smith, although there was hardly room or provisions for such an influx of visitors.

At the request of their beloved missionary, the Indians performed the laborious chore of clearing the land for the Dutch settlers. The influx of the Dutch, however, created friction between the new settlers and the Indians. The Indians had a long held custom of traveling south in order to hunt and fish, and it was during these forays that the Dutch would often seize the Indian's fields, corn, beans, as well as other belongings such as copper and brass kettles for their own use. Naturally, such actions were frowned upon by the Indians, thus creating the seeds of hostility between the two groups.

Less than one year after the arrival of the Dutch, relations between the two groups had deteriorated to the point that the Reverend Smith was compelled to begin the search for a new location for the colony. In the spring of 1848, George Smith, in the company of Chief Peter Waukazoo, departed Old Wing and proceeded northwards along the coast of Lake Michigan to survey possible sites for the colony's relocation. After having traveled as far north as the Straits of Mackinac, the party agreed upon a location in Leelanau County. After returning to Old Wing, the Indians immediately began preparations to abandon the mission for the move north. Following the decision to relocate, the land upon which the colony resided upon was sold to the Dutch settlers.[4]

The Indians departed Old Wing bound for their new home in canoes and Mackinaw boats. Meanwhile, the Reverend Smith and his family, along with the families of James McLaughlin and William Case boarded the schooner *Hiram Merrill*, which had been acquired in Chicago specifically for the relocation effort. Also aboard the 23-ton vessel were four cattle, three calves, and three horses.

Having endured years of harsh living conditions that defined the pioneering lifestyle, Arvilla Smith held some reservations about giving up her home and beginning anew in Leelanau

County. Evidence of this, along with the respect that the Indians felt towards George Smith and his family, can be found in the following excerpt from her writings done during the time of the abandonment of the Old Wing Mission:

> "The Indians began selling land and packing up for the north...to a place where Dutchmen couldn't find. The Chief came to me with an earnest appeal. ...'Your husband loves us and he is like our brother and you a sister. Where can we find anyone that will do for us as you have done? You won't say no, sister?' I told him I would go where my husband felt it his duty to go. What a hardship again, and my children pining for society! After all the suffering and privation of social privileges to again drag them into the wilderness and deprive them of what was dear as life. The sorrow of leaving my beautiful home and the graves of my children was great."[5]

Having survived a storm on the lake, the *Hiram Merrill* arrived in Grand Traverse Bay on June 12, 1849. Shortly after landing, the first Christian religious service ever performed in Leelanau County took place. In recognition of the party safely arriving at their destination, the Reverend Smith offered up a prayer of thanksgiving at this impromptu ceremony.

Following the settler's arrival at their new home, a temporary camp was established while work began on permanent structures nearby. All of the men belonging to the colony participated in the arduous task of cutting down trees and turning them into usable lumber. Although the frame for the Reverend Smith's log home was completed in one day, it was several weeks before it was ready to be occupied. While construction work continued, the schooner *Merrill* was sent to Traverse City to obtain additional building supplies.

In 1851, George Smith purchased roughly 200 acres of land that surrounded his house. Afterwards, he sent his son, George, Jr., to the nearest land office at Ionia to have the transaction recorded. During this same time, the founding of a village took place that was named Waukazooville, in honor of the Ottawa chief, Peter Waukazoo. This community would be known by this name until its renaming in 1854 to Northport.

The Reverend Smith reestablished the Old Wing Mission on the western shore of the Leelanau Peninsula about 2 ½ miles west of Waukazooville. Around the mission, at which a government school was built, a small Ottawa Indian village was settled and named Nomineseville.[6]

Soon after the establishment of this mission, George Smith was appointed as an official interpreter by the Government, a job that paid him an annual salary of $400 and a position he would retain throughout the balance of his life. As the population in the region expanded, the Reverend was called upon to serve in additional official capacities. This included serving as a probate judge, justice of the peace, a coroner, and Leelanau County's first treasurer.

George Smith's personal views concerning equality between the races was put to the test in 1851 when his oldest daughter, Mary, announced her intention to marry an Indian by the name of Payson Wolfe, who was the only son of Chief Miingun. Considering that the Smith children had grown up amongst the Native Americans, and had been taught to regard them as their equals, such a union was understandable.

Arvilla Smith, however, strongly objected to her daughter's marriage plans. Meanwhile, the Reverend Smith was confronted with the dilemma that a refusal to accept the marriage would go against the beliefs that he held dear. Furthermore, such a course of action would destroy all of the hard work he and his family had put towards building a relationship with the Indians during the preceding thirteen years.

In the end, George Smith supported his daughter's wishes, and officiated at her marriage ceremony on July 29, 1851. Following their marriage, Payson Wolfe built a home and began farming. During the Civil War, he fought for the Union Army until being captured during the Siege of Petersburg. After a brief stint of incarceration at the Libby Prison, the Confederacy transferred Payson to the infamous Andersonville Prison where he emerged, like many others, in a severely weakened state following the end of the war. The couple would go on to have thirteen children before Mary divorced Payson due to negative habits he acquired while serving in the war.[7]

Having disliked secretive organizations throughout most of his life, George Smith made the unlikely decision to join the Freemasons in 1869. Due to the prevailing distrust of that fraternal order, the Reverend's association with this group made him vulnerable to personal criticism from his peers. Such attacks prompted George Smith's decision to withdraw from the Congregational Association three years later and to unite the Old Wing Mission with the Presbyterian Board, a move opposed by many of the Indians belonging to the Mission. As such, he was replaced by the Reverend Barnard at Nomineseville and the Reverend Kirkland at Northport.

Later, however, a number of Indians attempted to restore their relations with George Smith. These efforts proved somewhat successful and led to a resumption of Mr. Smith preaching to his flock. These services took place six miles to the south of Northport at Omena, in a small Presbyterian church originally established by the Reverend Peter Dougherty to serve as the focal point of his work with the Indians.

Following a ten-day battle with Bright's disease, the Reverend George Smith died on April 5, 1881 at the age of 73 years old.[8] His funeral, which was held three days later, was attended not only by a large number of citizens living in the Northport area, but also by many Indians that in some cases had traveled over fifty miles in order to pay their last respects. George Smith was buried in a grave near his home. Arvilla Smith lived another fourteen years before dying on April 16, 1895, after which she was laid to rest next to her husband. During their life together, George and Arvilla Smith had endured countless hardships and challenges that were common in a missionary's life during the developmental period of the United States. The couple had ten children, six of which died either at birth or in their infancy.

Today, the village of Northport is a popular destination for vacationers. The community is surrounded by a number of cherry and apple orchards and has one of the finest marinas on Grand Traverse Bay. Occupying an area only equal to 1.75 square miles, Northport is the home to approximately 525 permanent residents.

# NOTES

## Chapter One
## Protecting a Vital Chokepoint

1. Bernie Arbic and Nancy Steinhouse. *Upbound Downbound: The Story of the Soo Locks* (Allegan Forest: The Priscilla Press, 2005), p. 21.

2. Ralph D. Williams. *The Honorable Peter White* (Cleveland, Ohio: Freshwater Press, 1986), p. 119.

3. Bernie Arbic and Nancy Steinhouse. *Upbound Downbound: The Story of the Soo Locks*, p. 37.

4. Lake Carriers' Association. *Lake Carriers' Association Annual Report - 1950* (Cleveland, Ohio: Lake Carriers' Association, 1951), p. 46.

5. Bernie Arbic and Nancy Steinhouse. *Upbound Downbound: The Story of the Soo Locks*, p. 49.

6. George J. Joachim. *Iron Fleet: The Great Lakes in World War II* (Detroit, Michigan: Wayne State Press, 1994), p. 60.

7. Arizona Republic, October 8, 1941.

8. The Charleston Daily Mail, October 8, 1941.

9. George J. Joachim. *Iron Fleet: The Great Lakes in World War II*, p. 64.

10. *Ibid.*, p. 65.

11. Bernie Arbic and Nancy Steinhouse. *Upbound Downbound: The Story of the Soo Locks*, p. 52.

12. The Carl D. Bradley sank in Lake Michigan on November 18, 1958, with the loss of 33 lives.

13. George J. Joachim. *Iron Fleet: The Great Lakes in World War II*, p. 69.

14. The News-Palladium, October 25, 1945.

15. Bernie Arbic and Nancy Steinhouse. *Upbound Downbound: The Story of the Soo Locks*, p. 56.

16. Lake Carriers' Association. *2010 Great Lakes Dry-Bulk Commerce Report*.

## Chapter Two
### The Midland Salt & Lumber Plant Explosion – 1892

1.  State of Michigan, Office of the State Inspector of Salt. *37th Annual Report of the State Inspector of Salt of Michigan - 1905.*
2.  Logansport Daily Reporter, May 13, 1892.
3.  *Ibid.*
4.  Oak Park Vindicator, March 25, 1892.

## Chapter Three
### Train Collision at Battle Creek - 1893

1.  Berenice Bryant Lowe. *Tales of Battle Creek.* (Battle Creek: Albert L. and Louise B. Miller Foundation, Inc., 1976), p. 147.
2.  *Ibid.*, p. 148.
3.  The New York Times, October 27, 1893.
4.  In many references, the engineer's name is spelled as Woolley. The spelling used here was obtained from reports concerning legal proceedings subsequent to the accident.
5.  The Evening Herald, October 20, 1893. Note: Some reports published at the time of the accident indicate that neither crew took action to slow or stop their respective trains before jumping.
6.  The New York Times, October 27, 1893.
7.  The Evening Herald, October 20, 1893.
8.  The New York Times, October 27, 1893.
9.  The Evening Herald, October 20, 1893.
10. The New York Times, October 27, 1893.
11. The Marshall Statesman, November 17, 1893.
12. The Daily Chronicle, November 16, 1893.

# Chapter Four
## Detroit Water Tunnel Explosion—1930

1. The Rhinelander Daily News, June 10, 1930.
2. Some sources estimate that there may have been 36 workers in the tunnel at the time.
3. Decatur Evening Herald, June 9, 1930.
4. Altoona Mirror, June 10, 1930.
5. The Owosso Argus-Press, June 10, 1930.


# Chapter Five
## The Osceola Mine Disaster—1895

1. The Weekly Wisconsin, September 21, 1895.
2. *Ibid.*
3. *Ibid.*
4. Mine Inspector's Report for Houghton County, Michigan; for the year ending September 30, 1895.
5. The Weekly Wisconsin, September 21, 1895.
6. *Ibid.*
7. *Ibid.*
8. The Gazette, September 13, 1895.
9. The Weekly Wisconsin, September 21, 1895.
10. *Ibid.*
11. Newspaper reports published at the time of the accident contain a wide range of spelling for many of the victims.
12. The Gazette, September 13, 1895.
13. Mine Inspector's Report for Houghton County, Michigan; for the year ending September 30, 1895.
14. An upcast shaft serves as a ventilation shaft for air after it has circulated through the mine. Meanwhile, a downcast shaft allows air to enter the mine.

# Chapter Six
## Surviving the Great Storm—1913

1. The Marine Historical Society of Detroit. *Ahoy & Farewell II.* (Detroit: The Marine Historical Society of Detroit, 1996), p. 43.

2. The cities of Fort William and Port Arthur, Ontario became collectively known as Thunder Bay on January 1, 1970 following the merger of these two communities.

3. In some sources, the captain's name is spelled as Hagen.

4. Frank Barcus. *Freshwater Fury.* (Detroit: Wayne State University Press, 1960), p. 46.

5. *Ibid.*, p.49.

6. Robert J. Hemming. *Ships Gone Missing.* (Chicago: Contemporary Books, 1992), p. 94-95.

7. The Waterloo Times-Tribune, November 15, 1913.

8. Robert J. Hemming. *Ships Gone Missing.* (Chicago: Contemporary Books, 1992), p. 96.

9. Mary Frances Doner. *The Salvager.* (Minneapolis: Ross and Haines, Inc., 1958), p. 150-151.

10. The Marine Historical Society of Detroit. *Great Lakes Ships We Remember II.* (Cleveland: Freshwater Press, Inc., 1984), p. 123.

11. John O. Greenwood. *Namesakes 1956-1980.* (Cleveland: Freshwater Press, Inc., 1981), p. 1.

# Chapter Seven
## A Name on a Tombstone

1. State of Michigan Adjutant General's Office. *Record of Service of Michigan Volunteers in the Civil War, 1861-1865, Volume # 3.* (Kalamazoo: Ihling Bros. & Everard, 1905).

2. *Ibid.*

3. Civil War Sites Advisory Committee (CWSAC), National Park Service. *Boydton Plank Road Battle Summary.*

4. Robert W. Waitt. *Official Publication #12: Libby Prison*. (Richmond: Richmond Civil War Centennial Committee, 1961-1965).

# Chapter Eight
## Stove Capital of the World

1. James J. Mitchell. *Detroit in History and Commerce*. (Detroit: Rogers & Thorpe, Publishers, 1891), p. 40.
2. *Ibid.*, p. 40.
3. *Ibid.*, p. 40.
4. The Homestead, October 3, 1907.
5. Willis Dunbar & George S. May. *Michigan: A History of the Wolverine State*. (Grand Rapids: Wm. B. Eerdmans Publishing Co., 1995), p. 412.
6. James J. Mitchell. *Detroit in History and Commerce*. (Detroit: Rogers & Thorpe, Publishers, 1891), p. 43.
7. *Ibid.*, p. 43.
8. Willis Dunbar & George S. May. *Michigan: A History of the Wolverine State*. (Grand Rapids: Wm. B. Eerdmans Publishing Co., 1995), p. 412.
9. The Detroit News, February 26, 1997.

# Chapter Nine
## The Struggle to Join Two Peninsulas

1. Lawrence A. Rubin. *Mighty Mac*. (Detroit: Wayne State University Press, 1986), p. 2.
2. Father Jacques Marquette is also commonly referred to as Pére (Father) Marquette.
3. In several ways, this cultural divide persists to this day.
4. Lawrence A. Rubin. *Mighty Mac*. (Detroit: Wayne State University Press, 1986), p. 8.
5. George W. Hilton. *The Great Lakes Car Ferries*. (Berkeley: Howell-North, 1962), p. 55.

6. Lawrence A. Rubin. "William Saulson – Michigan Pioneer," *Michigan Jewish History Volume 4 Number 1, November 1963*. (Detroit: Jewish Historical Society of Michigan, 1963), p. 3.

7. The News-Palladium, September 26, 1957.

8. Lawrence A. Rubin. *Mighty Mac*. (Detroit: Wayne State University Press, 1986), p. 9.

9. The News-Palladium, September 26, 1957.

10. The Marine Historical Society of Detroit. *Great Lakes Ships We Remember*. (Cleveland: Freshwater Press, Inc., 1979), p. 32.

11. The Ironwood Times, May 4, 1923.

12. The Appleton Post-Crescent, September 13, 1928.

13. Modjeski and Masters continue to provide bridge construction and refurbishment services.

14. The News-Palladium, August 10, 1940.

15. Ironwood Daily Globe, August 5, 1941.

16. The Ironwood Times, August 26, 1942.

17. Ironwood Daily Globe, October 23, 1941.

18. The Daily News, September 8, 1943.

19. Mr. Brown is recognized as the "Father of the Mackinac Bridge."

20. The difference between two amounts represents the distribution fees for the bonds.

21. Lawrence A. Rubin. *Mighty Mac*. (Detroit: Wayne State University Press, 1986), p. 26.

22. A press release issued by the Mackinac Bridge Authority, dated January 11, 2012, states that 3,728,896 vehicles crossed the bridge during 2011.

# Chapter Ten
## Michigan's Oldest Lighthouse

1. This vessel's name is often spelled as the *Griffin* in English.

2. Lucius Lyon later became one of Michigan's first US Senators in 1837.

3.  National Park Service. *Inventory of Historic Light Stations, Michigan Lighthouses*. Fort Gratiot Light Data Sheet.

4.  United States Coast Guard. *Light List, Volume VII, Great Lakes*. (Washington D. C.: U. S. Government Printing Office, 2012), p. 97.

## Chapter Eleven
### New Gnadenhutten

1.  Zauchtenthal is modern day Suchdol nad Odrou, Czech Republic.

2.  Henry A. Ford. "The Old Moravian Mission at Mount Clemens," *Collections and Researches made by the Pioneer Society of the State of Michigan, Volume 10*. (Lansing: Wynkoop Hallenbeck Crawford Company, 1908), p. 108.

3.  Some sources note the spelling of the Major's name as "DePeyster" or "de Peyster."

4.  Robert B. Ross & George B. Catlin. *Landmarks of Wayne County and Detroit*. (Detroit: The Evening News Association, 1898), p. 231.

5.  Patricia Schott Sawyer. "The Moravians and Richard Conner," *Mount Clemens Public Library, Local History Sketches*. (Mount Clemens: Mt. Clemens Public Library, 1980)

6.  Henry A. Ford. "The Old Moravian Mission at Mount Clemens," *Collections and Researches made by the Pioneer Society of the State of Michigan, Volume 10*. (Lansing: Wynkoop Hallenbeck Crawford Company, 1908), p. 111.

7.  Patricia Schott Sawyer. "The Moravians and Richard Conner," *Mount Clemens Public Library, Local History Sketches*. (Mount Clemens: Mt. Clemens Public Library, 1980)

8.  Henry A. Ford. "The Old Moravian Mission at Mount Clemens," *Collections and Researches made by the Pioneer Society of the State of Michigan, Volume 10*. (Lansing: Wynkoop Hallenbeck Crawford Company, 1908), p. 112.

9.  *Ibid.*, p. 108-112.

10. Patricia Schott Sawyer. "The Moravians and Richard Conner," *Mount Clemens Public Library, Local History Sketches*. (Mount Clemens: Mt. Clemens Public Library, 1980)

11. Henry A. Ford. "The Old Moravian Mission at Mount Clemens," *Collections and Researches made by the Pioneer Society of the State of Michigan, Volume 10*. (Lansing: Wynkoop Hallenbeck Crawford Company, 1908), p. 112-113.

12. *Ibid.*, p. 113.

13. Patricia Schott Sawyer. "The Moravians and Richard Conner," *Mount Clemens Public Library, Local History Sketches*. (Mount Clemens: Mt. Clemens Public Library, 1980)

14. Henry A. Ford. "The Old Moravian Mission at Mount Clemens," *Collections and Researches made by the Pioneer Society of the State of Michigan, Volume 10*. (Lansing: Wynkoop Hallenbeck Crawford Company, 1908), p. 113.

15. Some sources spell the Major's name as "Ancram."

16. Robert B. Ross & George B. Catlin. *Landmarks of Wayne County and Detroit*. (Detroit: The Evening News Association, 1898), p. 236-237.

# Chapter Twelve
## The Burning of Holland—1871

1. Despite its grievous loss of life, the Peshtigo Fire was overshadowed by the Great Chicago Fire and has become a largely forgotten disaster.

2. G. Van Schelven. "The Burning of Holland, October 9, 1871," *Report of the Pioneer Society of the State of Michigan, Volume 9*. (Lansing: Wynkoop Hallenbeck Crawford Company, 1908), p. 335.

3. *Ibid.*, p. 335.

4. *Ibid.*, p. 335-336.

5. *Ibid.*, p. 336.

6. *Ibid.*, p. 338.

# Chapter Thirteen
## Michigan's Most Unique Island

1. Lawrence M. Sommers (Editor). *Atlas of Michigan.* (Lansing: Michigan State University Press, 1977), p. 58.

2. B. S. Butler & W. S. Burbank. *The Copper Deposits of Michigan.* (Washington D. C.: United States Government Printing Office, 1929), p. 96.

3. There is a slight variation between sources as to the exact number of lives lost.

4. Julius F. Wolff, Jr. *Lake Superior Shipwrecks.* (Duluth: Lake Superior Port Cities, Inc., 1990), p. 199-200.

5. National Oceanic and Atmospheric Administration (NOAA). "S/S Kinsman Independent," *Incident News, November 25, 1990.*

6. The Detroit News, August 11, 1998.

7. The Webster's Dictionary defines an ossuary as a place or a receptacle for bones of the dead.

8. Ironwood Daily Globe, July 31, 1928.

9. In 1929, archeologist George A. West published the findings of the McDonald-Massee Expedition in a book titled *Copper: Its Mining and Use by the Aborigines of the Lake Superior Region.*

10. Idaho Evening News, August 9, 1937.

11. Star Tribune, June 15, 2012.

# Chapter Fourteen
## The Alpena Excursion Train Wreck—1902

1. Despite its name, the Detroit & Mackinac Railway never connected to Detroit during its nearly 100-year existence.

2. The Post-Standard, June 9, 1902.

3. "McKnight v. Detroit & M. RY. Co., Supreme Court of Michigan. January 5, 1904." *The Northwestern Reporter, Volume 97.* (St Paul: West Publishing Co., 1904), p. 773.

4. *Ibid.*, p. 773-774.

# Chapter Fifteen
## The Life of a Pioneering Missionary

1. Etta Smith Wilson. "Life and Work of the Late Rev. George N. Smith, a Pioneer Missionary." *Collections and Researches Made by the Michigan Pioneer and Historical Society, Volume 30.* (Lansing: Wynkoop Hallenbeck Crawford Company, 1906), p. 194.

2. *Ibid.*, p. 198.

3. *Ibid.*, p. 200.

4. Although some sources credit the fear of a smallpox epidemic as the motivation behind the colony's relocation, such a factor is not contained within the written account of Reverend Smith's life by Mr. Etta Smith Wilson.

5. The Holland Sentinel, August 29, 1999.

6. Etta Smith Wilson. "Life and Work of the Late Rev. George N. Smith, a Pioneer Missionary." *Collections and Researches Made by the Michigan Pioneer and Historical Society, Volume 30.* (Lansing: Wynkoop Hallenbeck Crawford Company, 1906), p. 207.

7. *Ibid.*, p. 209.

8. During the nineteenth century, the term Bright's disease was commonly used to describe a range of kidney disorders.

# BIBLIOGRAPHY

Arbic, Bernie & Steinhaus, Nancy. *Upbound Downbound: The Story of the Soo Locks.* Allegan Forest: The Priscilla Press, 2005.

Barcus, Frank. *Freshwater Fury.* Detroit: Wayne State University Press, 1960.

Butler, B. S. & Burbank, W. S. *The Copper Deposits of Michigan.* Washington D.C.: United States Government Printing Office, 1929.

Doner, Mary Frances. *The Salvager.* Minneapolis: Ross & Haines, Inc., 1958.

Dunbar, Willis F. & May, George S. *Michigan: A History of the Wolverine State.* Grand Rapids: Wm. B. Eerdmans Publishing Co., 1995.

Ford, Henry A. "The Old Moravian Mission at Mount Clemens," *Collections and Researches of the Pioneer Society of the State of Michigan.* Lansing: Wynkoop Hallenbeck Crawford Company, 1908.

Greenwood, John O. *Namesakes 1956-1980.* Cleveland: Freshwater Press, Inc., 1981.

Havighurst, Walter. *The Long Ships Passing.* New York: Macmillan Publishing Co., Inc., 1975.

Hemming, Robert J. *Ships Gone Missing.* Chicago: Contemporary Books, Inc., 1992.

Hilton, George W. *The Great Lakes Car Ferries.* Berkeley: Howell-North, 1962.

Joachim, George J. *Iron Fleet: The Great Lakes in World War II.* Detroit: Wayne State University Press, 1994.

Lake Carriers' Association. *Lake Carriers' Association Annual Report – 1950.* Cleveland: Lake Carriers' Association, 1951.

Lowe, Berenice Bryant. *Tales of Battle Creek.* Battle Creek: Albert L. and Louise B. Miller Foundation, Inc., 1976.

Mitchell, James J. *Detroit in History and Commerce.* Detroit: Rogers & Thorpe, Publishers, 1891.

Powers, Perry F. *A History of Northern Michigan and its People, Volume 1.* Chicago: The Lewis Publishing Company, 1912.

Ross, Robert B. & Catlin, George B. *Landmarks of Wayne County and Detroit.* Detroit: The Evening News Association, 1898.

Rubin, Lawrence A. *Mighty Mac.* Detroit: Wayne State University Press, 1986.

Schelven, G. Van. "The Burning of Holland, October 9, 1871," *Report of the Pioneer Society of the State of Michigan.* Lansing: Wynkoop Hallenbeck Crawford Company, 1908.

Sommers, Lawrence M. (Editor) *Atlas of Michigan.* Lansing: Michigan State University Press, 1977.

State of Michigan Adjutant General's Office. *Record of Service of Michigan Volunteers in the Civil War, 1861-1865, Volume # 3.* Kalamazoo: Ihling Bros. & Everard, 1905.

The Marine Historical Society of Detroit. *Ahoy & Farewell II.* Detroit: Marine Historical Society of Detroit, Inc., 1996.

——. *Great Lakes Ships We Remember.* Cleveland: Freshwater Press, Inc., 1979.

——. *Great Lakes Ships We Remember II*.  Cleveland: Freshwater Press, Inc., 1984.

Waitt, Robert W.  *Official Publication #12: Libby Prison*.  Richmond: Richmond Civil War Centennial Committee, 1961-1965.

Williams, Ralph D.  *The Honorable Peter White*.  Cleveland: Freshwater Press, Inc., 1986.

Wilson, Etta Smith.  "Life and Work of the Late Rev. George N. Smith, a Pioneer Missionary."  *Collections and Researches Made by the Michigan Pioneer and Historical Society, Volume 30*.  Lansing: Wynkoop Hallenbeck Crawford Company, 1906.

Wolff, Julius F., Jr.  *Lake Superior Shipwrecks*.  Duluth: Lake Superior Port Cities, Inc., 1990.

# INDEX

# Index